THE COSMOLOGICAL ARGUMENTS

DONALD R. BURRILL is Associate Professor of Philosophy at California State College at Los Angeles and holds a Ph.D. from the University of Southern California. He is the author of several articles in academic journals in Philosophy of Law and Philosophy of Religion.

THE COSMOLOGICAL ARGUMENTS

A Spectrum of Opinion

EDITED BY DONALD R. BURRILL

ANCHOR BOOKS
DOUBLEDAY & COMPANY, INC.
GARDEN CITY, NEW YORK
1967

The Anchor Books edition is the first
publication of *The Cosmological Arguments*

Anchor Books edition: 1967

CONTENTS

discusses the ontological argument

THE COSMOLOGICAL ARGUMENTS

INTRODUCTION

The authors of the essays in this anthology are concerned with a common question: Is there rational evidence for the existence of God? Some of the selections support the thesis that there is such evidence, others deny it; but whether they affirm or deny this premise, these "theistic proofs" continue to evoke philosophical interest for many.

The reader will discover that the arguments in this volume provide sufficient divergency of opinion to foster rousing philosophical dialogue, so it is hardly necessary for the Introduction to review all phases of the controversy. Therefore, I shall concentrate on two aspects of the struggle. First, it will be worth while for us to consider the present state of these "rational arguments," and second, it may be useful to set forth what presently seem to be the general areas of criticism.

But the arguments await appraisal by the reader alone, for it is he who must finally determine for himself whether they confirm religious conviction or strengthen agnosticism.

I

It is customary to divide "theistic proofs" into *a priori* and *a posteriori* arguments. The *a priori* arguments begin with intrinsic autonomous premises and end, it is supposed, with the logically warranted conclusion: "Therefore, God exists." The most noteworthy *a priori* form is, of course, the *ontological* argument.[1] But the essays that follow are occupied with the *a posteriori* forms, and specifically with those traditionally characterized as *cosmological*.

The premises of *a posteriori* arguments are derived, not from self-evident or intrinsic assumptions, but rather from human experience; and the conclusions reached are judged to follow rationally from that experience. These arguments begin with observable effects and attempt to establish the cause that initiates these effects. In their *cosmological* form (which is truly paradigmatic for *a posteriori* arguments), the arguments draw on a specific aspect of the universe and, then, with reference to a set of general laws, proceed to demonstrate the existence of God.

It is St. Thomas Aquinas (1225–74), building in spectacular fashion on the philosophical theology of his predecessors, who is credited with formulation of the four basic cosmological forms.[2] He designates these forms *motion, cause, contingency,* and *design.* They begin with certain "brute facts" about the universe, namely, its permanence, change, reality, and order, and derive from these elements evidence *a posteriori* for God's existence. Let us look at each in detail.

(1) The argument that begins with the indubitability of *motion* is surely one of the oldest "proofs" in rational theology. It first appears in the tenth book of

---

[1] For an extensive analysis of the ontological argument, see Alvin Plantinga, ed., *The Ontological Argument, from St. Augustine to Contemporary Philosophers* (New York, 1965).

[2] Aquinas actually gives us five, but the fourth "way" is not clearly cosmological.

Plato's *Laws*. That account, however, is extremely simplistic. The entire argument turns on the motion of animated objects. An animate object is self-moving, while an inanimate object moves only when moved by some animate source. The Sophists, Plato's intellectual adversaries, had assumed that living things spring from the inanimate, and that matter is the incipient ground of everything else.[3] Plato rejects such a conception, arguing instead that inanimate things are never (logically or chronologically) prior to animate objects, because the inanimate is always dependent upon a spontaneous or internally initiated source for its movement. It cannot move itself.[4] Accordingly, the source of motion can be only that which has the power of motion within itself. This Plato conceived as "mind" or "soul" —the singular element that exists prior to and causes movement in all inanimate objects. That is the extent of Plato's argument, and it alone constitutes his theological case for "soul" as the source of motion. The remainder of the discussion is spent demonstrating, at least to his own satisfaction, that "soul" is *Soul* (God or Gods) because the magnitude of motion in the universe necessitates a Soul of cosmic proportions. Since Plato's argument also lends itself to teleological consideration, which will be investigated in due course, we need not pursue it further here.

Aristotle, who undoubtedly produced the most interesting theological arguments in Greek philosophy, accepts the Platonic dictum that motion is evidence for God, but he does not accept the additional doctrine

[3] See Plato's *Phaedrus*.
[4] An argument that Walter Kaufmann rightly maintains is based on the hidden premise that rest is natural and motion is unnatural (one might say transnatural). *Critique of Religion and Philosophy* (New York, 1958), Chapter V.

that God *is* motion. He concedes that God is the source
of motion, but God must remain unmoved. It cannot
be otherwise, for if God moves, then he becomes
changing being—hence contingent—and contingency is
logically incompatible with immutability. In other
words, a mutable God might possibly not exist. God,
in order to be the source of all change, must always
exist; and that which always exists is, at least to that
degree, immutable. Therefore, God is Unmoved
Mover.[5]

The nerve of this argument begins with two simple
factual experiences. First, there is change—nothing is
more evident. Second, things that change are never the
cause of their own change—at least this is true of all
human experience. All change in the world, so to
speak, is determined by preceding changes.[6] Everything that is changed is moved to that change by another—*D* is moved and so is changed by the action of
C, and *C* by action of *B,* and *B* by *A*. But eventually
one must account for the prime source of change, that
is, original motion. This, however, is metaphysically
puzzling, for the initial mover, let us say *A,* must, if it
is truly prime, be distinguished from the acts *B, C,*
and *D;* it cannot be the consequence of any prior act,
but must be the active agent of all other acts while
remaining itself unchanged. It is logically necessary
that *A* exist; for if there were no initial mover, then
there would be no motion or change at all, since all
present action is subsequent to the actions of prior
agents that are themselves never self-changing. Thus

---

[5] *Metaphysics,* Book VIII.

[6] Even atomic particles, for example, that may seem self-
changing because they function as self-contained objects of
matter and energy, cannot be self-changing since their initial
appearance is dependent upon a determining change.

A as mover but not moved, while rationally necessary, is obviously not common to our present experience, so must be an agent of transnatural rather than of natural order. In the words of Aquinas, "This everyone understands to be God."

To this initial explanation, however, the contemporary apologist adds two qualifying principles. First, the concept of cosmological motion is never limited to *local* motion. That is, motion is not restricted to sequential places or spaces, but is defined metaphysically as any form of change. This is the process of moving from one state of being to another (from potency to act, as the Scholastics would have it); for example, the change of child into man or of water into steam. In other words, the change that comes about is not to be interpreted as a causal chain of events, on the order of falling dominoes, but is envisioned as a complex connection between various states of being, preserved and supported by a prime metaphysical state of Being.

The second qualifying principle follows logically from the first, namely, if motion is not to be restricted to particular objects moving from one point in space and time to another, then insistence upon temporal sequence has no particular significance and may very well be misleading. Prime Mover is not only the initial member in a temporal series, but, more significantly, the highest metaphysical order of Being to which all other changing agents are subordinate. P. T. Geach suggests that the proper analogue for Prime Mover is more correctly a "minstrel as the source of music" than it is a "blacksmith as the source of a shoe." The number of moving agents that are interjected between the unmoved first mover and present motion is irrelevant. Therefore, the issue of infinite series is quite beside the point, since the first mover is not limited to the sole task of activating phenomena in temporal sequence, but is the overriding ontological foundation for the total world process.

(2) Aquinas' second basic cosmological form parallels the first argument. It begins with our common experiences about efficient cause and proceeds, even as does the previous argument, from the empirical fact of change to the cause of change. It is an obvious fact of experience not only that objects move, but also that we are surrounded by a constellation of conditions that are as they are because of a multitude of causal events. Moreover, it is apparent that these events act as the causal nexuses of future events, and the links in the web of cause spread in every direction.

This form of the argument rests on three tenets concerning *cause*—two that are commonplace and a third that is assumed to be rationally demonstrable. First, it is obvious that this world is a network of events that are the result of interdependent causal occurrences. Secondly, analysis reveals that these events do not cause themselves. And finally—a tenet not so obvious—there can be no infinite causal chain. It is necessary to postulate an initial cause. This claim requires considerable investigation. According to its proponents, if one assumes an infinite series of efficient causes while rejecting the principle of first cause, he is assuredly caught in contradiction. For without initial cause, there is no way for the act of causality to be imparted to changing events; a cause cannot produce what it must necessarily have imparted to it. An efficient cause simply cannot impart action to itself. There must be a "superior" principle, a "self-causing cause" one may say, and again, this "everyone understands to be God."

Notice that causality under these conditions is interpreted in terms of metaphysics, not physics. The argument claims that everything in the temporal order is in the process of "becoming," *potentia est ad actum*— moving from potential being of transitory form to actualized being in final form. Man, as "finite knower," most commonly understands his experience as a series of efficient causes in continuous finite moments; that is, he is inclined to interpret the world of objects as becoming and passing away. But metaphysical analysis reveals that causality is considerably more than sequential physical explanation. Hume, for one, had argued that cause requires temporal priority. But such a conception—causality in temporal sequence (*in fieri*) —is only a partial description, for causality is also continuous act (*in esse*). For instance, death at the hand of an assassin is causality in temporal sequence, but the process of photosynthesis is not, since photosynthesis is the conservation of continuing effects brought about by the sun in synthesis with organic elements. In this relationship, causal priority is hardly appropriate, for photosynthesis is not a series that requires the impulses of previous events, but rather a process of enduring occurrences that preserves the present state of affairs.

(3) Perhaps the most interesting cosmological form, however, is the *contingency* argument, which incorporates the two prior forms, since it draws on both permanence and change. The argument asserts that everything that exists contingently need not exist, while everything that exists by necessity must exist. It is obvious that this is a contingent world—a world obedient to kaleidoscopic change and eventual destruction, a world of things that exist now, but in the future will not.

In fact, the thought that most of the world we presently experience need not have existed as it does at all is perfectly comprehensible. All that presently is could easily not have been, or could easily not be tomorrow. Such an idea is comprehensible because contingent objects are dependent upon occurrences that cannot be brought about by the contingent state itself. If events prior to the present situation had occurred differently, then the present state of things, obviously, would have been different. And since it is perfectly possible to envision a world otherwise than it presently is, it is also possible to envision an entirely different world having different causal patterns and producing differing states of affairs. But this possibility raises two questions: first, are the events upon which contingent things depend, themselves contingent? And second, if so, does this imply that experience is made up of an infinite series of contingent states?

The argument's apologists contend that if both questions are answered affirmatively, then once again the conception of reality becomes contradictory since such an account leaves unexplained why anything exists at all. If every present contingent state depends on a previous occurrence, and if that prior state is itself contingent, and so *ad infinitum,* then adequate explanation of their causality is not provided. Moreover, if these contingent events happen in sequential order and occur within the context of infinite time, then at the present moment there should be nothing at all; because everything contingent within the span of infinity will, at some particular moment, not exist.

Hence, for there to be anything contingent in the universe, there must be at least one thing that is not contingent—something that is, as the Scholastics urged, *necessary* throughout all change and is self-established. A necessary being exists of itself and logically cannot perish. Moreover, it is not dependent upon anything else, but is, was, and always will be. Again, in the words of Aquinas: this being men conceived to be "God."

(4) This now brings us to the final cosmological form, traditionally called the *teleological* argument, which has been the most popular from Plato onward. The argument maintains that from the fact of *design* that is so obviously manifested in the world, it is possible to conclude that the design has an "intelligent purposeful" source. There is in the universe a pattern of means-occurrences that eventuates in particular ends. And no accounting of the means-end process in non-rational objects, save intelligent source, seems feasible, except the bold appeal to chance; and such an appeal is never an explanation, but the abandonment of explanation.

In order to draw together the various aspects of this argument, consider the following metaphorical account. On a hot, sultry day, a swimmer decides to take a dip in the ocean; but upon arriving at the shore he finds that he must descend a seventy-foot precipice to reach the water. However, because the day is very hot, he is not deterred and sets about to discover a way of descent. Investigation proves to his delight that there is a series of foot-size rocks in descending order from the top of the cliff to the ocean below, and without hesitation he descends to the invigorating water. Only after swimming does he pause to evaluate his good fortune philosophically. The question arises in his mind: are those rock stairs here fortuitously, or by intelligent plan? Is my swim sheer good fortune, or has someone else seeking descent prepared the rocks on another occasion? Observing the rocks closely reveals noticeable subtleties that indicate order, or what would appear to be order. Nevertheless, this order alone need not lead one to the conclusion that someone has placed the rocks as they are. But one thing is certain—no matter what the order of the rocks, they themselves cannot determine their particular position on the cliff wall, for they lack the power of intelligent action. Suppose, then, that the swimmer is convinced that the rocks' *de facto* design requires an intelligent purposing agent. The fact of design alone is not sufficient to establish the case for such an agent. The swimmer is also obliged to answer Hume's assertion that the appearance of design may very well be a schema that the observer himself is imposing on the rocks. To offset that objection, he is forced to show, not only that the order in the rocks exhibits intelligent design, but also that the design is telic, that is, that it indicates an intended end or final purpose. Hence, for the observer to conclude that the rocks are placed purposely and not fortuitously, it is necessary to discover in their orderliness an overriding structure that accounts for their particular function within a total rational scheme. In this particular metaphor, there must be evidence that another individual has had reason also to descend from the cliff rim to the water. The emphasis on *end* or *intention* is absolutely necessary if the defenders of the teleological argument are to escape the claim that the order is merely imposed upon the phenomenon by the observer.

Furthermore, the principle of goal-direction provides the teleologist with a much needed reply to those critics who claim that the notion of design is being interpreted in reverse order, that it is precisely because things are so constructed that they obtain the particular goals they do, rather than that they are so constructed in order to attain the goals. Ostensively, the design and the purposed ends that lace the fabric of the universe as a whole are more than sufficient indications to the teleologist that there is an intelligent source directing all things toward intended goals.

These four forms, then—*motion, efficient cause, contingency,* and *order*—constitute the principal features of the cosmological arguments. They may be summarized in the following syllogism:

(a) This is an orderly universe whose existence and order require rational explanation.

(b) We experience in the universe a changing structure that is the result of numerous prior causes; and these causes, it is agreed, constitute adequate explanation for every change and its particular structure.

(c) The universe of itself, however, cannot produce initial change, that is, it cannot change from the state of non-existence to the state of existence.

(d) Nor can it be regarded as having existed infinitely, since total and continuous changeableness entails the possibility of passing out of existence (within the span of infinite time).

(e) *Therefore,* the present order and every change within the composition of the universe rest upon an initial or prime source that is in itself unchangeable (uncaused); it is Being of a higher metaphysical order, a rationally necessary Being (God) whose non-existence is inconceivable.

II

These arguments have carried, and continue to carry, for many, considerable significance as "proofs."

But the conviction that they are indeed "proofs" has been lost, I fear, on the majority of the philosophical community.

For those already convinced of God's existence on other grounds, the cosmological arguments will more than likely support, and perhaps strengthen, their convictions; but for those not committed to such belief, the arguments seem less than conclusive. This is not to say that one could not be convinced by them, but only that they contain no inexorable logical force or rational inevitability—even though it is this supposed irresistability their defenders have always stressed.

But putting these conjectures aside, it will be useful to review the principal areas of criticism. The critical essays in the volume can be separated into three types. There are, first, those objections calling into question the truth value of logical, as opposed to empirical, evidence; second, those objections raising doubt about the tacit metaphysical notions that these arguments assume; and third, those objections stressing the confusion resulting from undesignated referents. Let us consider each general area.

(1) Most contemporary philosophers insist on the distinction made by Leibniz between "proof" in a strictly logical sense, as self-evident necessity, and "proof" in the sense of probable occurrence. In the former case, a premise in an argument is a part of a formally valid set of assertions from which one derives a valid conclusion. This form of "proof" need not establish the factual accuracy of any of its assertions. On the other hand, "proof" as probable occurrence is derived from empirically produced experiences that are subject to the test of reasonable judgment. Explanation as probable occurrence is never self-evident. It is always vulnerable to debatable interpre-

tations of those experiences that are regarded as its "brute facts."

One of the objections to the cosmological arguments involves these two conceptions of "proof." Are these arguments intended to provide logically inevitable conclusions, in the sense that mathematics provides valid conclusions from a set of mathematical assertions (analytical propositions)? Or do they supply us only with probable conclusions that can be challenged by numerous sets of contrary probability assertions (synthetic propositions)? Or are we to conclude that no significant distinction is to be made between analytic and synthetic assertions, because the arguments are intended to include both methods?

It is clear enough that, at least in their present form, the arguments are not exclusively analytic. If they depended entirely upon the formal method, then proof would be assured—but only at the expense of triviality, for a purely analytical proof, in this instance, would beg the question at stake. Consider the following elementary example. It is logically permissible to argue p and (if p, then q), therefore q; that is, given the true statement p (the world exists) and if statement p, then statement q (God exists), therefore, the conclusion q (God exists) is true. This formulation is logically irreproachable, for one cannot affirm the premises and at the same time deny the conclusion; but it is obvious that one may remain unconvinced about the truth of the compounded premises p and (if p, then q), because there is nothing self-evident about the factual relationship between p and q. Surely anyone who acknowledges a true connection between p and q has already assumed what he intends to demonstrate. Therefore, those who accept the cosmological arguments as "proofs" have in mind considerably more than an exercise in tautological argumentation. How much more is the critical issue.

On the other hand, it is unquestionably true that these arguments are regarded as confirmable in an *a posteriori* sense. Those who support them insist that it is rationally legitimate to conclude from the direct experience of permanence, change, and order that everything is the created product of God. But is it also true that these arguments are intended to be *merely* probable? Are they probable in a statistical sense? I think not, for the conception of God's existence is not intended to hang on the probable or improbable reasonableness of the evidence, that is, "proof" as statistical chance.[7] Moreover, statistical probability includes the principle of prediction; and prediction is hardly applicable to the claims of a necessary "first cause," since there is no way to test the predicted expectations.

I judge, then, that the arguments are regarded as having, in some degree, both the self-evidence of mathematical propositions, and the factual confirmation of empirical experience.

But it is precisely the conditions of analytic necessity and probable occurrence that cannot be fulfilled simultaneously. If we begin with the factual premise that there is a universe, and conclude that this necessarily entails a prior entity as its source, we are advocating a proof—not in any empirically demonstrable sense, but totally on definitional grounds—that not having a "first cause" is inconceivable. But in what sense is it inconceivable? The argument begins as *a posteriori* and then is turned around and confirmed as an *a priori* logical requirement, that is, it is impos-

---

[7] Although the teleological form of the argument may very well rest, at least in part, on the notion of reasonable probability.

sible to have contingent events unless there is an initial necessary source. But is this not, as Kant warned, the ontological argument once again? For its truth claim is based not on empirical premises, but rather on the hitherto suppressed premise that empirical contingency is feasible only on the condition that it is the result of a Being that cannot be contingent. This is surely not an empirical premise, and must be accepted, if at all, as a self-evident postulate.

The first general objection, then, rejects the so-called "rational necessity" that is adjudged to accompany these arguments. The arguments rightly demonstrate that contingency fails to supply the intellectual inevitability that all formal "proofs" demand; but unhappily, existential events are such that no matter where one seeks "proof" for them—at the beginning of time or the end of time, or supervening the entire process—one is never led to confirm them as intrinsically necessary.

(2) The second general objection questions the claim that the universe is rationally explicable. The assertion that the universe implies a God because it is ultimately rational is, at the least, a metaphysical assumption open to question. John Hick suggests, for example, that the cosmological arguments are logically defensible only because they rule out the possibility that the world may be ultimately inexplicable. But are there philosophical grounds for such a conclusion? There are no logical grounds for it. The notion that the universe is ultimately "rational" rests not on the nature of rational necessity, but on an individual's fundamental belief that it is so—that is, on an act of faith alone.[8]

---

[8] *The Existence of God* (New York, 1964), p. 6. Perhaps the word "faith" carries too great a theological load in this context.

There is common support for this conclusion in modern philosophy, from Hume to Sartre. Hume's astounding attack on the entire question of necessary connection quite naturally compounds the difficulty that one has in making the common notion of ordinary causality conceptually plausible. Furthermore, Kant's insistence that the fabric of all rational experience contains elements that are the domain of the mind alone, throws additional doubt on the classical character of causal reality. Most contemporary philosophers do not flag in their conviction that questions about the ultimate cause of the universe remain a mystery quite beyond the powers of philosophical investigation. Sartre believes that the universe is "gratuitous." Russell sees the question as submerged in meaningless verbiage, and is content to declare that the universe is "just there and that's all."[9]

The essence of this second objection, then, is that a question about necessary first cause is significant if one takes a particular metaphysical position about reality. Such a position is itself not rationally inevitable, nor is it the only option available.

(3) The final objection in some respects entails the other two—or, perhaps more accurately, the preceding objections presuppose the third. It calls into question the meaningfulness of the arguments by contending that they seek answers to nonsensical questions. This objection would fix a linguistic veto on the entire enterprise.

I confess that I find myself in considerable agreement with the linguistic method—though I am not convinced that the objections leveled against these

9 A debate on the existence of God with F. C. Copleston, 1948. Reprinted, Bertrand Russell, *Why I Am Not a Christian* (London, 1957), Chapter 13.

"proofs" accomplish as much as their advocates hope, since the entire problem of verifying evidence continues to need clarification. Nevertheless, whether or not one subscribes to the verification procedure of linguistic philosophy, these objections warrant considerably more attention than they have received in theology and religion.[10]

In sum, we may say that these objections take two forms. First, they evoke doubt about the meaningfulness of the questions that the cosmological arguments attempt to answer; and second, they question the terminological referents that these arguments seem to presuppose. According to the first criticism, the questions are improper, although they seem to be meaningful. They are grammatically sensible, and because of ordinary usage seem understandable; in fact, it is customary application that provokes the confusion. Consider the following questions: Where is the sun? or moon? or Cassiopeia? These questions are clearly meaningful because it is possible to establish a conceptual structure in which they may be answered. The answers are found, obviously, in a relational framework that includes other astronomical bodies and the galaxical system of which they are a part. But the question "Where is the universe?" is oddly non-sensical. It may seem to have the same conceptual answer as the question "Where is the sun?" but in fact does not. The sun question entails, quite properly, multiple objects in relation to each other, and all these objects within the boundaries of space. But the same question applied to the universe is not answerable, be-

[10] I believe that the "Death of God" controversy reflects a growing awareness of these issues on the part of theologians. See Paul Van Buren, *The Secular Meaning of the Gospel* (New York, 1963).

cause it has no relation to other "universes," or location in relation to other "locations." It has no fixed point, so to speak, from which one can draw a defining line connecting other points outside the universe. The notion of "location" is no more appropriate to the universe than is a conception of its speed or direction of travel.

Now the same criticism is applicable to the cosmological arguments. For example, it is a requirement that every cosmological "proof" resolve the question of "origin," but a question about origin requires an explanation that falls outside the sensible boundaries applicable to the term "universe." For the universe *in toto* has no specifiable relationship to events or occurrences outside itself. The term "origin" is no more significant for the universe than are the terms "location," "speed," and "direction" (at least in the light of our present state of physical description).

The upshot is that some questions that are perfectly sensible within subseries are not applicable to the total series. This phase of the linguistic objection maintains that the term "universe" is not intended to be applied to an object that requires an origin. Therefore, no analogue that includes the word "comes from" adds to our present understanding of the term.

The second form of the linguistic objection is directed at certain theological terms and their hard-to-discover referents. Take as an example the crucial word "God" itself. This word requires every bit as much analysis as do assertions about existence; for if the terminological issue is ignored, it is difficult to understand just how a claim of "proof" is to be applied to the conception of existence. Without agreement on the constant referent "God," it is impossible to judge what counts as confirming or disconfirming his existence. At one time or another, theologians have defined God as "superhuman," "super-mind," "organic process," "hydrogen particle," "everything," "nothing," and so on; but the word remains an enigma to its philosophical critics. If, for instance, it is agreed that the term "Napoleon" stands for "The Emperor of France in A.D. 1805" (one of numerous definitional options), then a series of inductive inferences that determine if it is or is not the case are applicable. If the statement is accurate, evidence can be produced, some of which would be, for example, spatial and temporal, and would support the assertion that Napoleon was Emperor of France—specifically, that he did occupy a space (France) and a moment (1805) on the face of this planet.

In similar fashion, if it is argued that the term "God" refers to "Divine Being," and this "Being," in part, exhibits "manlike" characteristics, then many of the inductive procedures similar to those applicable to Napoleon's existence are also applicable to God's. If God is (at least analogically) a being with mental and physical characteristics, a perfect personal being who can be spoken of (to put it crudely) as residing above the earth somewhere out beyond the galaxical systems, then we do have some notion as to what kind of experience would constitute evidence of his existence.

But the term's very ambiguity, in some degree, has been responsible for the philosophical claim that the statement "God exists" is a solecism, whose occurrence is brought about because reality (existence) is attached to a term (God) for which there is no meaningful instance. Clarification of this issue, then, might very well help to alleviate an aspect of current linguistic criticism. Usually, however, the terminological question is never resolved, and the meaning of the word "God" is merely assumed. William James, using a quotation from Professor James Henry Leuba, writes, "God is not known, he is not understood, he is used . . . ask no more than that . . ."[11]

It is this terminological confusion, I believe, that is partially implied in Paul Tillich's assertion that the

> . . . question of the existence of God can be neither asked nor answered. If asked, it is a question about that which by its very nature is above existence, and therefore the answer—whether negative or affirmative —implicitly denies the nature of God. It is as atheistic to affirm the existence of God as it is to deny it.[12]

Tillich seems to be warning against postulating a God of quasi-corporeal dimensions that exists along with other "things" in the universe; and if this notion is conceded, that is, if God does not exist in a "thinglike" manner, then theologians must pause to consider the entire conception of God, and in particular, the traditional assumptions that are made. The issue then becomes: Is it possible to have a meaningful referent for the term "God"?

Perhaps, then, one of the most significant contributions of linguistic analysis is to have demonstrated that the starting point for the philosophy of religion is not God's existence, but an acceptable definition of the term "God."[13]

These objections constitute the three most impell-

[11] *The Varieties of Religious Experience* (New York, 1902), Lecture XX.

[12] *Systematic Theology* (Chicago, 1955), Vol. I, p. 237.

[13] The "God," however, that the arguments in this volume presuppose, it may be generally said, is an eternal, uncreated, and personal being who has created everything and exercises love, mercy, and justice toward mankind.

ing criticisms that are presently brought against the cosmological arguments, and they are objections that rational theology has not fully met. Therefore, it seems to me that support of the cosmological arguments demands more philosophical optimism than is warranted, and I am inclined to agree with those who find it inappropriate to seek resolution to these questions by means of rational "proof." The traditional forms of philosophical argumentation do not provide the "reasons" that will bring us nearer to a knowledge of God. God must be found in some other way.

III

A brief word concerning the format of the book may be helpful. It is divided into three parts: Part I concentrates on the cosmological arguments of motion, cause, and contingency, followed by the critique of these arguments. Part I(C) offers some current discussion on the issue. Part II limits analysis to the teleological form of the arguments and then turns to the classical criticisms of Hume and Kant. Part II(C) concludes with several contemporary discussions, both supporting and denying the arguments. And Part III offers three essays, each of which reflects a different philosophical mood about the particular state and significance of the cosmological arguments in current philosophical theology.

PART I

THE COSMOLOGICAL ARGUMENT

A. THE CLASSICAL VIEW

1. PLATO (428–348? B.C.)

[The *Laws,* the longest of Plato's dialogues and one
of the last, is an ingenious expression of natural or
philosophical theology. Plato, convinced that Theism is
capable of scientific demonstration, offers one of the
earliest forms of the cosmological argument. In Book
X, the *Athenian Stranger* (perhaps modeled after
Plato) sets before *Cleinias* (a minor Cretan official)
the elements of the argument. The issue turns on an
analysis of motion and change. Everything that moves
either moves itself or is moved by something else. It is
either internal and spontaneous or external and inert.
Anything that exhibits spontaneous motion is *alive*—it
is, Plato insists, "soul" (ψυχή), "the motion that
moves itself." Now soul, Cleinias concedes, as a self-
moving mover must be logically prior to every other
form of reality and the necessary cause of all external,
but not self-moved, forms. Therefore, the superior and
prime cause of everything that moves is living soul—
in other words, God (or perhaps gods).]

Motion and Change as a Rational Demonstration of God*

[1] The soul through all her being is immortal, for that
which is ever in motion is immortal; but that which
moves another and is moved by another, in ceasing to

* Selections from *Phaedrus* and *Laws,* Jowett translation.
[1] First paragraph only from *Phaedrus* 245 c.

move ceases also to live. Only the self-moving, never leaving itself, never ceases to move, and is the fountain and beginning of motion to all that moves besides. Now, the beginning is unbegotten, for that which is begotten has a beginning; but the beginning is begotten of nothing, for if it were begotten of something, then the begotten would not come from a beginning. But if unbegotten, it must also be indestructible; for if beginning were destroyed, there could be no beginning out of anything, nor anything out of a beginning; and all things must have a beginning. And therefore the self-moving is the beginning of motion; and this can neither be destroyed nor begotten, else the whole heavens and all creation would collapse and stand still, and never again have motion or birth. But if the self-moving is proved to be immortal, he who affirms that self-motion is the very idea and essence of the soul will not be put to confusion. For the body which is moved from without is soulless; but that which is moved from within has a soul, such motion being inherent in the soul. . . .

Cleinias. What do you mean?

Athenian Stranger. I mean this: when one thing changes another, and that another, of such will there be any primary changing element? How can a thing which is moved by another ever be the beginning of change? Impossible. But when the self-moved changes other, and that again other, and thus thousands upon tens of thousands of bodies are set in motion, must not the beginning of all this motion be the change of the self-moving principle?

Cleinias. Very true, and I quite agree.

Athenian Stranger. Or, to put the question in another way, making answer to ourselves:—If, as most of these philosophers have the audacity to affirm, all things were at rest in one mass, which of the above-mentioned principles of motion would first spring up among them?

Cleinias. Clearly the self-moving; for there could be no change in them arising out of any external cause; the change must first take place in themselves.

Athenian Stranger. Then we must say that self-motion being the origin of all motions, and the first which arises among things at rest as well as among things in motion, is the eldest and mightiest principle of change, and that which is changed by another and yet moves other is second.

Cleinias. Quite true.

Athenian Stranger. At this stage of the argument let us put a question.

Cleinias. What question?

Athenian Stranger. If we were to see this power existing in any earthy, watery, or fiery substance, simple or compound—how should we describe it?

Cleinias. You mean to ask whether we should call such a self-moving power life?

Athenian Stranger. I do.

Cleinias. Certainly we should.

Athenian Stranger. And when we see soul in anything, must we not do the same—must we not admit that this is life?

Cleinias. We must.

Athenian Stranger. And now, I beseech you, reflect; —you would admit that we have a threefold knowledge of things?

Cleinias. What do you mean?

Athenian Stranger. I mean that we know the essence, and that we know the definition of the essence,

and the name,—these are the three; and there are two
questions which may be raised about anything.

Cleinias. How two?

Athenian Stranger. Sometimes a person may give the
name and ask the definition; or he may give the definition and ask the name. I may illustrate what I mean
in this way.

Cleinias. How?

Athenian Stranger. Number like some other things is
capable of being divided into equal parts; when thus
divided, number is named 'even,' and the definition of
the name 'even' is 'number divisible into two equal
parts'?

Cleinias. True.

Athenian Stranger. I mean, that when we are asked
about the definition and give the name, or when we
are asked about the name and give the definition—in
either case, whether we give name or definition, we
speak of the same thing, calling 'even' the number
which is divided into two equal parts.

Cleinias. Quite true.

Athenian Stranger. And what is the definition of that
which is named 'soul'? Can we conceive of any other
than that which has been already given—the motion
which can move itself?

Cleinias. You mean to say that the essence which is
defined as the self-moved is the same with that which
has the name soul?

Athenian Stranger. Yes; and if this is true, do we
still maintain that there is anything wanting in the
proof that the soul is the first origin and moving power
of all that is, or has become, or will be, and their contraries, when she has been clearly shown to be the
source of change and motion in all things?

Cleinias. Certainly not; the soul as being the source

of motion, has been most satisfactorily shown to be the oldest of all things.

Athenian Stranger. And is not that motion which is produced in another, by reason of another, but never has any self-moving power at all, being in truth the change of an inanimate body, to be reckoned second, or by any lower number which you may prefer?

Cleinias. Exactly.

Athenian Stranger. Then we are right, and speak the most perfect and absolute truth, when we say that the soul is prior to the body, and that the body is second and comes afterwards, and is born to obey the soul, which is the ruler?

Cleinias. Nothing can be more true.

Athenian Stranger. Do you remember our old admission, that if the soul was prior to the body the things of the soul were also prior to those of the body?

Cleinias. Certainly.

Athenian Stranger. Then characters and manners, and wishes and reasonings, and true opinions, and reflections, and recollections are prior to length and breadth and depth and strength of bodies, if the soul is prior to the body.

Cleinias. To be sure.

Athenian Stranger. In the next place, must we not of necessity admit that the soul is the cause of good and evil, base and honourable, just and unjust, and of all other opposites, if we suppose her to be the cause of all things?

Cleinias. We must.

Athenian Stranger. And as the soul orders and inhabits all things that move, however moving, must we not say that she orders also the heavens?

Cleinias. Of course.

Athenian Stranger. One soul or more? More than

one—I will answer for you; at any rate, we must not suppose that there are less than two—one the author of good, and the other of evil.

Cleinias. Very true.

Athenian Stranger. Yes, very true; the soul then directs all things in heaven, and earth, and sea by her movements, and these are described by the terms—will, consideration, attention, deliberation, opinion true and false, joy and sorrow, confidence, fear, hatred, love, and other primary motions akin to these; which again receive the secondary motions of corporeal substances, and guide all things to growth and decay, to composition and decomposition, and to the qualities which accompany them, such as heat and cold, heaviness and lightness, hardness and softness, blackness and whiteness, bitterness and sweetness, and all those other qualities which the soul uses, herself a goddess, when truly receiving the divine mind she disciplines all things rightly to their happiness; but when she is the companion of folly, she does the very contrary of all this. Shall we assume so much, or do we still entertain doubts?

Cleinias. There is no room at all for doubt.

Athenian Stranger. Shall we say then that it is the soul which controls heaven and earth, and the whole world?—that it is a principle of wisdom and virtue, or a principle which has neither wisdom nor virtue? Suppose that we make answer as follows:—

Cleinias. How would you answer?

Athenian Stranger. If, my friend, we say that the whole path and movement of heaven, and of all that is therein, is by nature akin to the movement and revolution and calculation of mind, and proceeds by kindred laws, then, as is plain, we must say that the best soul takes care of the world and guides it along the good path.

Cleinias. True.

Athenian Stranger. But if the world moves wildly and irregularly, then the evil soul guides it.

Cleinias. True again.

Athenian Stranger. Of what nature is the movement of mind?—To this question it is not easy to give an intelligent answer; and therefore I ought to assist you in framing one.

Cleinias. Very good.

Athenian Stranger. Then let us not answer as if we would look straight at the sun, making ourselves darkness at midday,—I mean as if we were under the impression that we could see with mortal eyes, or know adequately the nature of mind;—it will be safer to look at the image only.

Cleinias. What do you mean?

Athenian Stranger. Let us select of the ten motions[2] the one which mind chiefly resembles; this I will bring to your recollection, and will then make the answer on behalf of us all.

Cleinias. That will be excellent.

Athenian Stranger. You will surely remember our saying that all things were either at rest or in motion?

Cleinias. I do.

Athenian Stranger. And that of things in motion some were moving in one place, and others in more than one?

Cleinias. Yes.

Athenian Stranger. Of these two kinds of motion, that which moves in one place must move about a

---

[2] Just prior to this selection, Plato has listed ten forms of motion, nine external and inert, one self-moved.

center like globes made in a lathe, and is most entirely akin and similar to the circular movement of mind.

Cleinias. What do you mean?

Athenian Stranger. In saying that both mind and the motion which is in one place move in the same and like manner, in and about the same, and in relation to the same, and according to one proportion and order, and are like the motion of a globe, we invented a fair image, which does no discredit to our ingenuity.

Cleinias. It does us great credit.

Athenian Stranger. And the motion of the other sort which is not after the same manner, nor in the same, nor about the same, nor in relation to the same, nor in one place, nor in order, nor according to any rule or proportion, may be said to be akin to senselessness and folly?

Cleinias. That is most true.

Athenian Stranger. Then, after what has been said, there is no difficulty in distinctly stating, that since soul carries all things round, either the best soul or the contrary must of necessity carry round and order and arrange the revolution of the heaven.

Cleinias. And judging from what has been said, Stranger, there would be impiety in asserting that any but the most perfect soul or souls carries round the heavens.

Athenian Stranger. You have understood my meaning right well, Cleinias, and now let me ask you another question.

Cleinias. What are you going to ask?

Athenian Stranger. If the soul carries round the sun and moon, and the other stars, does she not carry round each individual of them?

Cleinias. Certainly.

Athenian Stranger. Then of one of them let us speak, and the same argument will apply to all.

Cleinias. Which will you take?

Athenian Stranger. Every one sees the body of the sun, but no one sees his soul, nor the soul of any other body living or dead; and yet there is great reason to believe that this nature, unperceived by any of our senses, is circumfused around them all, but is perceived by mind; and therefore by mind and reflection only let us apprehend the following point.

Cleinias. What is that?

Athenian Stranger. If the soul carries round the sun, we shall not be far wrong in supposing one of three alternatives.

Cleinias. What are they?

Athenian Stranger. Either the soul which moves the sun this way and that, resides within the circular and visible body, like the soul which carries us about every way; or the soul provides herself with an external body of fire or air, as some affirm, and violently propels body by body; or thirdly, she is without such a body, but guides the sun by some extraordinary and wonderful power.

Cleinias. Yes, certainly; the soul can only order all things in one of these three ways.

Athenian Stranger. And this soul of the sun, which is therefore better than the sun, whether taking the sun about in a chariot to give light to men, or acting from without, or in whatever way, ought by every man to be deemed a God.

Cleinias. Yes, by every man who has the least particle of sense.

Athenian Stranger. And of the stars too, and of the moon, and of the years and months and seasons, must we not say in like manner, that since a soul or souls having every sort of excellence are the causes of all of them, those souls are Gods, whether they are living beings and reside in bodies, and in this way order the whole heaven, or whatever be the place and mode of their existence;—and will any one who admits all this venture to deny that all things are full of Gods?

Cleinias. No one, Stranger, would be such a madman.

2. ARISTOTLE (384–322 B.C.)

Aristotle, as Plato, argues that theology is scientifically demonstrable. He is committed to a description of God that is derived from a series of inferences based on the consistency principle in nature. Two points should be emphasized: first, Aristotle considers "theology" the necessary conclusion for physics. It is the transcendent end (τέλος) toward which all motion is directed, the final goal of natural order. Second, to Christianize Aristotle's God is misleading. There is not a shred of mysticism in these arguments, and God is never concerned with either the Universe or its inhabitants. God is an intellectual necessity, not an object of worship. But it should not be assumed that Aristotle was totally insensitive to questions of personal religion. His early descriptions are filled with religious expressions. Moreover, it is interesting that he, along with Plato and Kant, finds the starry heavens a panoply impelling enough to evoke belief in divine beings.]

The Necessary Existence of a First Mover*

But evidently there *is* a first principle, and the causes of things are neither an infinite series nor infinitely various in kind. For neither can one thing proceed

* From *The Basic Works of Aristotle*, edited by Richard McKeon (New York, 1941). Reprinted by permission of the Clarendon Press, Oxford, and Random House, Inc. *Metaphysics*, Books II, XII.

from another, as from matter, *ad infinitum* (e.g. flesh from earth, earth from air, air from fire, and so on without stopping), nor can the sources of movement form an endless series (man for instance being acted on by air, air by the sun, the sun by Strife,[1] and so on without limit). Similarly the final causes cannot go on *ad infinitum*—walking being for the sake of health, this for the sake of happiness, happiness for the sake of something else, and so one thing always for the sake of another. And the case of the essence is similar. For in the case of intermediates, which have a last term and a term prior to them, the prior must be the cause of the later terms. For if we had to say which of the three is the cause, we should say the first; surely not the last, for the final term is the cause of none; nor even the intermediate, for it is the cause only of one. (It makes no difference whether there is one intermediate or more, nor whether they are infinite or finite in number.) But of series which are infinite in this way, and of the infinite in general, all the parts down to that now present are alike intermediates; so that if there is no first there is no cause at all. . . .

Since there were[2] three kinds of substance, two of them physical and one unmovable, regarding the latter we must assert that it is necessary that there should be an eternal unmovable substance. For substances are the first of existing things, and if they are all destructible, all things are destructible. But it is impossible that movement should either have come into being or cease to be (for it must always have existed), or that time should. For there could not be a before and an after

[1] The illustration is taken from the cosmology of Empedocles.
[2] Cf. 1069a30.

if time did not exist. Movement also is continuous, then, in the sense in which time is; for time is either the same thing as movement or an attribute of movement. And there is no continuous movement except movement in place, and of this only that which is circular is continuous.

But if there is something which is capable of moving things or acting on them, but is not actually doing so, there will not necessarily be movement; for that which has a potency need not exercise it. Nothing, then, is gained even if we suppose eternal substances, as the believers in the Forms do, unless there is to be in them some principle which can cause change; nay, even this is not enough, nor is another substance besides the Forms enough; for if it is not to *act,* there will be no movement. Further, even if it acts, this will not be enough, if its essence is potency; for there will not be *eternal* movement, since that which is potentially may possibly not be. There must, then, be such a principle, whose very essence is actuality. Further, then, these substances must be without matter; for they must be eternal, if *anything* is eternal. Therefore they must be actuality.

Yet there is a difficulty; for it is thought that everything that acts is able to act, but that not everything that is able to act acts, so that the potency is prior. But if this is so, nothing that is need be; for it is possible for all things to be capable of existing but not yet to exist.

Yet if we follow the theologians who generate the world from night, or the natural philosophers who say that 'all things were together',[3] the same impossible result ensues. For how will there be movement, if there

[3] Anaxagoras.

is no actually existing cause? Wood will surely not move itself—the carpenter's art must act on it; nor will the menstrual blood nor the earth set themselves in motion, but the seeds must act on the earth and the *semen* on the menstrual blood.

This is why some suppose eternal actuality—e.g. Leucippus[4] and Plato[5]; for they say there is always movement. But why and what this movement is they do not say, nor, if the world moves in this way or that, do they tell us the cause of its doing so. Now nothing is moved at random, but there must always be something present to move it; e.g. as a matter of fact a thing moves in one way by nature, and in another by force or through the influence of reason or something else. (Further, what sort of movement is primary? This makes a vast difference.) But again for Plato, at least, it is not permissible to name here that which he sometimes supposes to be the source of movement—that which moves itself;[6] for the soul is later, and coeval with the heavens, according to his account.[7] To suppose potency prior to actuality, then, is in a sense right, and in a sense not; and we have specified these senses. That actuality is prior is testified by Anaxagoras (for his 'reason' is actuality) and by Empedocles in his doctrine of love and strife, and by those who say that there is always movement, e.g. Leucippus. Therefore chaos or night did not exist for an infinite time, but the same things have always existed (either passing through a cycle of changes or obeying some other law), since actuality is prior to potency. If, then, there is a constant cycle, something

[4] Cf. *De Caelo* iii. 300b8.
[5] Cf. *Timaeus* 30 A.
[6] Cf. *Phaedrus* 245 C; *Laws* 894 E.
[7] Cf. *Timaeus* 34 B.

must always remain,[8] acting in the same way. And if there is to be generation and destruction, there must be something else[9] which is always acting in different ways. This must, then, act in one way in virtue of itself, and in another in virtue of something else—either of a third agent, therefore, or of the first. Now it must be in virtue of the first. For otherwise this again causes the motion both of the second agent and of the third. Therefore it is better to say 'the first'. For it was the cause of eternal uniformity; and something else is the cause of variety, and evidently both together are the cause of eternal variety. This, accordingly, is the character which the motions actually exhibit. What need then is there to seek for other principles?

Since (1) this is a possible account of the matter, and (2) if it were not true, the world would have proceeded out of night and 'all things together' and out of non-being, these difficulties may be taken as solved. There is, then, something which is always moved with an unceasing motion, which is motion in a circle; and this is plain not in theory only but in fact. Therefore the first heaven[10] must be eternal. There is therefore also something which moves it. And since that which is moved and moves is intermediate, there is something which moves without being moved, being eternal, substance, and actuality. And the object of desire and the object of thought move in this way; they move without being moved. The primary objects of desire and of thought are the same. For the apparent good is the object of appetite, and the real good is the primary

[8] i. e. the sphere of the fixed stars.

[9] i. e. the sun. Cf. *De Gen. et Corr.* ii. 336a23 ff.

[10] i. e. the outer sphere of the universe, that in which the fixed stars are set.

object of rational wish. But desire is consequent on opinion rather than opinion on desire; for the thinking is the starting-point. And thought is moved by the object of thought, and one of the two columns of opposites is in itself the object of thought; and in this, substance is first, and in substance, that which is simple and exists actually. (The one and the simple are not the same; for 'one' means a measure, but 'simple' means that the thing itself has a certain nature.) But the beautiful, also, and that which is in itself desirable are in the same column; and the first in any class is always best, or analogous to the best.

That a final cause may exist among unchangeable entities is shown by the distinction of its meanings. For the final cause is (*a*) some being for whose good an action is done, and (*b*) something at which the action aims; and of these the latter exists among unchangeable entities though the former does not. The final cause, then, produces motion as being loved, but all other things move by being moved.

Now if something is moved it is capable of being otherwise than as it is. Therefore if its actuality is the primary form of spatial motion, then in so far as it is subject to change, in *this* respect it is capable of being otherwise—in place, even if not in substance. But since there is something which moves while itself unmoved, existing actually, this can in no way be otherwise than as it is. For motion in space is the first of the kinds of change, and motion in a circle the first kind of spatial motion; and this the first mover *produces*.[11] The first mover, then, exists of necessity; and in so far as it

---

[11] If it had any movement, it would have the first. But it produces this and therefore cannot share in it; for if it did, we should have to look for something that is prior to the first mover and imparts this motion to it.

exists by necessity, its mode of being is good, and it is in this sense a first principle. For the necessary has all these senses—that which is necessary perforce becaušе it is contrary to the natural impulse, that without which the good is impossible, and that which cannot be otherwise but can exist only in a single way.

On such a principle, then, depend the heavens and the world of nature. And it is a life such as the best which we enjoy, and enjoy for but a short time (for it is ever in this state, which we cannot be), since its actuality is also pleasure. (And for this reason[12] are waking, perception, and thinking most pleasant, and hopes and memories are so on account of these.) And thinking in itself deals with that which is best in itself, and that which is thinking in the fullest sense with that which is best in the fullest sense. And thought thinks on itself because it shares the nature of the object of thought; for it becomes an object of thought in coming into contact with and thinking its objects, so that thought and object of thought are the same. For that which is *capable* of receiving the object of thought, i. e. the essence, is thought. But it is *active* when it *possesses* this object. Therefore the possession rather than the receptivity is the divine element which thought seems to contain, and the act of contemplation is what is most pleasant and best. If, then, God is always in that good state in which we sometimes are, this compels our wonder; and if in a better this compels it yet more. And God *is* in a better state. And life also belongs to God; for the actuality of thought is life, and God is that actuality; and God's self-dependent actuality is life most good and eternal. We say therefore that God is a living being, eternal, most good,

[12] *sc.* because they are activities or actualities.

so that life and duration continuous and eternal belong to God; for this *is* God.

Those who suppose, as the Pythagoreans[13] and Speusippus[14] do, that supreme beauty and goodness are not present in the beginning, because the beginnings both of plants and of animals are *causes,* but beauty and completeness are in the *effects* of these,[15] are wrong in their opinion. For the seed comes from other individuals which are prior and complete, and the first thing is not seed but the complete being; e.g. we must say that before the seed there is a man—not the man produced from the seed, but another from whom the seed comes.

It is clear then from what has been said that there is a substance which is eternal and unmovable and separate from sensible things. It has been shown also that this substance cannot have any magnitude, but is without parts and indivisible (for it produces movement through infinite time, but nothing finite has infinite power; and, while every magnitude is either infinite or finite, it cannot, for the above reason, have finite magnitude, and it cannot have infinite magnitude because there is no infinite magnitude at all). But it has also been shown that it is impassive and unalterable; for all the other changes are posterior to[16] change of place.

It is clear, then, why these things are as they are. But we must not ignore the question whether we have to suppose one such substance or more than one, and

[13] Cf. 1075a36.

[14] Cf. vii. 1028b21, xiv. 1091a34, 1092a11.

[15] i. e. the animal or plant is more beautiful and perfect than the seed.

[16] i. e. impossible without.

if the latter, how many; we must also mention, regarding the opinions expressed by others, that they have said nothing about the number of the substances that can even be clearly stated. For the theory of Ideas has no special discussion of the subject; for those who speak of Ideas say the Ideas are numbers, and they speak of numbers now as unlimited, now[17] as limited by the number 10; but as for the reason why there should be just so many numbers, nothing is said with any demonstrative exactness. We however must discuss the subject, starting from the presuppositions and distinctions we have mentioned. The first principle or primary being is not movable either in itself or accidentally, but produces the primary eternal and single movement. But since that which is moved must be moved by something, and the first mover must be in itself unmovable, and eternal movement must be produced by something eternal and a single movement by a single thing, and since we see that besides the simple spatial movement of the universe, which we say the first and unmovable substance produces, there are other spatial movements—those of the planets—which are eternal (for a body which moves in a circle is eternal and unresting; we have proved these points in the physical treatises[18]), each of *these* movements also must be caused by a substance both unmovable in itself and eternal. For the nature of the stars[19] is eternal just because it is a certain kind of substance, and the mover is eternal and prior to the moved, and that which is prior to a substance must be a substance. Evidently, then, there must be substances which are of the

[17] The reference is to Plato (Cf. *Phys.* 206b32).
[18] Cf. *Phys.* viii. 8, 9; *De Caelo* i. 2, ii. 3–8.
[19] This is to be understood as a general term including both fixed stars and planets.

same number as the movements of the stars, and in their nature eternal, and in themselves unmovable, and without magnitude, for the reason before mentioned.[20]

That the movers are substances, then, and that one of these is first and another second according to the same order as the movements of the stars, is evident. But in the number of the movements we reach a problem which must be treated from the standpoint of that one of the mathematical sciences which is most akin to philosophy—viz. of astronomy; for this science speculates about substance which is perceptible but eternal, but the other mathematical sciences, i.e. arithmetic and geometry, treat of no substance. That the movements are more numerous than the bodies that are moved is evident to those who have given even moderate attention to the matter; for each of the planets has more than one movement. But as to the actual number of these movements, we now—to give some notion of the subject—quote what some of the mathematicians say, that our thought may have some definite number to grasp; but, for the rest, we must partly investigate for ourselves, partly learn from other investigators, and if those who study this subject form an opinion contrary to what we have now stated, we must esteem both parties indeed, but follow the more accurate.

Eudoxus supposed that the motion of the sun or of the moon involves, in either case, three spheres, of which the first is the sphere of the fixed stars, and the second moves in the circle which runs along the middle of the zodiac, and the third in the circle which is inclined across the breadth of the zodiac; but the circle in which the moon moves is inclined at a greater angle

[20] Cf. ll. 5–11.

than that in which the sun moves. And the motion of the planets involves, in each case, four spheres, and of these also the first and second are the same as the first two mentioned above (for the sphere of the fixed stars is that which moves all the other spheres, and that which is placed beneath this and has its movement in the circle which bisects the zodiac is common to all), but the *poles* of the third sphere of each planet are in the circle which bisects the zodiac, and the motion of the fourth sphere is in the circle which is inclined at an angle to the equator of the third sphere; and the poles of the third sphere are different for each of the other planets, but those of Venus and Mercury are the same.

Callippus made the position of the spheres the same as Eudoxus did, but while he assigned the same number as Eudoxus did to Jupiter and to Saturn, he thought two more spheres should be added to the sun and two to the moon, if one is to explain the observed facts; and one more to each of the other planets.

But it is necessary, if all the spheres combined are to explain the observed facts, that for each of the planets there should be other spheres (one fewer than those hitherto assigned) which counteract those already mentioned and bring back to the same position the outermost sphere of the star which in each case is situated below[21] the star in question; for only thus can all the forces at work produce the observed motion of the planets. Since, then, the spheres involved in the movement of the planets themselves are—eight for Saturn and Jupiter and twenty-five for the others, and of these only those involved in the movement of the lowest-situated planet need not be counteracted, the

---

[21] i. e. inwards from, the universe being thought of as a system of concentric spheres encircling the earth.

spheres which counteract those of the outermost two planets will be six in number, and the spheres which counteract those of the next four planets will be sixteen; therefore the number of all the spheres—both those which move the planets and those which counteract these—will be fifty-five. And if one were not to add to the moon and to the sun the movements we mentioned, the whole set of spheres will be forty-seven in number.

Let this, then, be taken as the number of the spheres, so that the unmovable substances and principles also may probably be taken as just so many; the assertion of *necessity* must be left to more powerful thinkers. But if there can be no spatial movement which does not conduce to the moving of a star, and if further every being and every substance which is immune from change and in virtue of itself has attained to the best must be considered an end, there can be no other being apart from these we have named, but this must be the number of the substances. For if there are others, they will cause change as being a final cause of movement; but there cannot *be* other movements besides those mentioned. And it is reasonable to infer this from a consideration of the bodies that are moved; for if everything that moves is for the sake of that which is moved, and every movement belongs to something that is moved, no movement can be for the sake of itself or of another movement, but all the movements must be for the sake of the stars. For if there is to be a movement for the sake of a movement, this latter also will have to be for the sake of something else; so that since there cannot be an infinite regress, the end of every movement will be one of the divine bodies which move through the heaven.

(Evidently there is but one heaven. For if there are

many heavens as there are many men, the moving principles, of which each heaven will have one, will be one in form but in *number* many. But all things that are many in number have matter; for one and the same definition, e. g. that of man, applies to many things, while Socrates is one. But the primary essence has not matter; for it is complete reality. So the unmovable first mover is one both in definition and in number; so too, therefore, is that which is moved always and continuously; therefore there is one heaven alone.)

Our forefathers in the most remote ages have handed down to their posterity a tradition, in the form of a myth, that these bodies are gods and that the divine encloses the whole of nature. The rest of the tradition has been added later in mythical form with a view to the persuasion of the multitude and to its legal and utilitarian expediency; they say these gods are in the form of men or like some of the other animals, and they say other things consequent on and similar to these which we have mentioned. But if one were to separate the first point from these additions and take it alone—that they thought the first substances to be gods, one must regard this as an inspired utterance, and reflect that, while probably each art and each science has often been developed as far as possible and has again perished, these opinions, with others, have been preserved until the present like relics of the ancient treasure. Only thus far, then, is the opinion of our ancestors and of our earliest predecessors clear to us.

The nature of the divine thought involves certain problems; for while thought is held to be the most divine of things observed by us, the question how it must be situated in order to have that character involves difficulties. For if it thinks of nothing, what is there

here of dignity? It is just like one who sleeps. And if it thinks, but this depends on something else, then (since that which is its substance is not the act of thinking, but a potency) it cannot be the best substance; for it is through thinking that its value belongs to it. Further, whether its substance is the faculty of thought or the act of thinking, what does it think of? Either of itself or of something else; and if of something else, either of the same thing always or of something different. Does it matter, then, or not, whether it thinks of the good or of any chance thing? Are there not some things about which it is incredible that it should think? Evidently, then, it thinks of that which is most divine and precious, and it does not change; for change would be change for the worse, and this would be already a movement. First, then, if 'thought' is not the act of thinking but a potency, it would be reasonable to suppose that the continuity of its thinking is wearisome to it. Secondly, there would evidently be something else more precious than thought, viz. that which is thought of. For both thinking and the act of thought will belong even to one who thinks of the worst thing in the world, so that if this ought to be avoided (and it ought, for there are even some things which it is better not to see than to see), the act of thinking cannot be the best of things. Therefore it must be of itself that the divine thought thinks (since it is the most excellent of things), and its thinking is a thinking on thinking.

But evidently knowledge and perception and opinion and understanding have always something else as their object, and themselves only by the way. Further, if thinking and being thought of are different, in respect of which does goodness belong to thought? For to *be* an act of thinking and to *be* an object of thought are not the same thing. We answer that in some cases the knowledge is the object. In the productive sciences it is the substance or essence of the object, matter omitted, and in the theoretical sciences the definition or the act of thinking is the object. Since, then, thought and the object of thought are not different in the case of things that have not matter, the divine thought and its object will be the same, i.e. the thinking will be one with the object of its thought.

3. St. Thomas Aquinas (1224–74)

[St. Thomas is doubtless the most significant theologian of the Middle Ages and justly deserves the title of "Angelic Doctor" that Catholic Christianity reserves for him, for he, more than anyone else, drew together the desultory notions of prior theology. In Aquinas, the contention that God's existence is an empirical fact—initially advanced by Plato and Aristotle—reaches fruition. But while for Plato and Aristotle theology is a minor issue that emerges from physics, for St. Thomas it is physics that is an appendage of theology. Nevertheless, Aquinas regards two of Aristotle's conceptions as beyond dispute: first, the universe is essentially rational and hence the logical and creative result of a divine agent; second, it is a purposely structured universe and knowledge about it is teleological in character. The reader will note that the fifth "way" in the following selections is teleological. This has been included here instead of in Part II because it was felt that a division of the "Five Ways" would be harmful to their literary quality, and little would be gained through their separation.]

*God Demonstrated Through His Effects.**

WHETHER GOD EXISTS?

We proceed thus to the Third Article:—

Objection 1. It seems that God does not exist; because if one of two contraries be infinite, the other would be altogether destroyed. But the name *God* means that He is infinite goodness. If, therefore, God existed, there would be no evil discoverable; but there is evil in the world. Therefore God does not exist.

Obj. 2. Further, it is superfluous to suppose that what can be accounted for by a few principles has been produced by many. But it seems that everything we see in the world can be accounted for by other principles, supposing God did not exist. For all natural things can be reduced to one principle, which is nature; and all voluntary things can be reduced to one principle, which is human reason, or will. Therefore there is no need to suppose God's existence.

On the contrary, It is said in the person of God: *I am Who am* (*Exod.* iii. 14).

I answer that, The existence of God can be proved in five ways.

The first and more manifest way is the argument from motion. It is certain, and evident to our senses, that in the world some things are in motion. Now whatever is moved is moved by another, for nothing can be moved except it is in potentiality to that towards which

* From *Introduction to St. Thomas Aquinas,* edited by Anton C. Pegis (New York, 1948). Reprinted by permission of Random House, Inc. and Burns & Oates, Ltd., London. *Summa Theologica,* Q. 2. Art. 3.

it is moved; whereas a thing moves inasmuch as it is in act. For motion is nothing else than the reduction of something from potentiality to actuality. But nothing can be reduced from potentiality to actuality, except by something in a state of actuality. Thus that which is actually hot, as fire, makes wood, which is potentially hot, to be actually hot, and thereby moves and changes it. Now it is not possible that the same thing should be at once in actuality and potentiality in the same respect, but only in different respects. For what is actually hot cannot simultaneously be potentially hot; but it is simultaneously potentially cold. It is therefore impossible that in the same respect and in the same way a thing should be both mover and moved, *i.e.*, that it should move itself. Therefore, whatever is moved must be moved by another. If that by which it is moved be itself moved, then this also must needs be moved by another, and that by another again. But this cannot go on to infinity, because then there would be no first mover, and, consequently, no other mover, seeing that subsequent movers move only inasmuch as they are moved by the first mover; as the staff moves only because it is moved by the hand. Therefore it is necessary to arrive at a first mover, moved by no other; and this everyone understands to be God.

The second way is from the nature of efficient cause. In the world of sensible things we find there is an order of efficient causes. There is no case known (neither is it, indeed, possible) in which a thing is found to be the efficient cause of itself; for so it would be prior to itself, which is impossible. Now in efficient causes it is not possible to go on to infinity, because in all efficient causes following in order, the first is the cause of the intermediate cause, and the intermediate is the cause of the ultimate cause, whether the

intermediate cause be several, or one only. Now to
take away the cause is to take away the effect. Therefore, if there be no first cause among efficient causes,
there will be no ultimate, nor any intermediate, cause.
But if in efficient causes it is possible to go on to infinity, there will be no first efficient cause, neither will
there be an ultimate effect, nor any intermediate efficient causes; all of which is plainly false. Therefore
it is necessary to admit a first efficient cause, to which
everyone gives the name of God.

The third way is taken from possibility and necessity, and runs thus. We find in nature things that are
possible to be and not to be, since they are found to
be generated, and to be corrupted, and consequently,
it is possible for them to be and not to be. But it is
impossible for these always to exist, for that which
can not-be at some time is not. Therefore, if everything
can not-be, then at one time there was nothing in existence. Now if this were true, even now there would
be nothing in existence, because that which does not
exist begins to exist only through something already
existing. Therefore, if at one time nothing was in existence, it would have been impossible for anything to
have begun to exist; and thus even now nothing would
be in existence—which is absurd. Therefore, not all beings are merely possible, but there must exist something the existence of which is necessary. But every
necessary thing either has its necessity caused by another, or not. Now it is impossible to go on to infinity
in necessary things which have their necessity caused
by another, as has been already proved in regard to
efficient causes. Therefore we cannot but admit the
existence of some being having of itself its own necessity, and not receiving it from another, but rather caus-

ing in others their necessity. This all men speak of as God.

The fourth way is taken from the gradation to be found in things. Among beings there are some more and some less good, true, noble, and the like. But *more* and *less* are predicated of different things according as they resemble in their different ways something which is the maximum, as a thing is said to be hotter according as it more nearly resembles that which is hottest; so that there is something which is truest, something best, something noblest, and, consequently, something which is most being, for those things that are greatest in truth are greatest in being, as it is written in *Metaph.* ii.[1] Now the maximum in any genus is the cause of all in that genus, as fire, which is the maximum of heat, is the cause of all hot things, as is said in the same book.[2] Therefore there must also be something which is to all beings the cause of their being, goodness, and every other perfection; and this we call God.

The fifth way is taken from the governance of the world. We see that things which lack knowledge, such as natural bodies, act for an end, and this is evident from their acting always, or nearly always, in the same way, so as to obtain the best result. Hence it is plain that they achieve their end, not fortuitously, but designedly. Now whatever lacks knowledge cannot move towards an end, unless it be directed by some being endowed with knowledge and intelligence; as the arrow is directed by the archer. Therefore some intelligent being exists by whom all natural things are directed to their end; and this being we call God.

Reply Obj. 1. As Augustine says: *Since God is the*

[1] *Metaph.* Ia, 1 993b30.
[2] *Ibid.*, 993b25.

highest good, He would not allow any evil to exist in His works, unless His omnipotence and goodness were such as to bring good even out of evil.[3] This is part of the infinite goodness of God, that He should allow evil to exist, and out of it produce good.

Reply Obj. 2. Since nature works for a determinate end under the direction of a higher agent, whatever is done by nature must be traced back to God as to its first cause. So likewise whatever is done voluntarily must be traced back to some higher cause other than human reason and will, since these can change and fail; for all things that are changeable and capable of defect must be traced back to an immovable and self-necessary first principle, as has been shown.

[3] *Enchir.* XI (PL 40, 236).

P. T. Geach's Commentary on Aquinas

[Peter T. Geach is professor of philosophy at the University of Leeds. The analysis that follows is a helpful commentary on St. Thomas' astonishingly compact set of rational arguments for the existence of God. Professor Geach devotes his initial remarks to the concept of "Maker and Sustainer of the World," before turning to the issue of divine existence. This is a valuable procedure, since Aquinas' precise conception of God circumscribes the logically possible "proofs." Moreover, it enables interpreters to understand correctly the basis of St. Thomas' rational evidence. For example, Professor Geach shows that Aquinas did not intend to prove the existence of God by tracing backward a series of generations that terminates in a Divine Being. Rather Aquinas treats the world as a total object, and the conception of total object stimulates a series of perfectly legitimate questions. What brought the world into existence? What keeps it from perishing as some of its parts perish? What keeps the processes going on? And to what end? The answers to these questions are met in a metaphysically necessary Being—God.]

including its whole time

Commentary on Aquinas*

In proving the existence of God, Aquinas shows a certain distaste for what may be called philosophical-sounding arguments—e.g. arguments based on our having an idea of a greatest or most perfect being, or on the existence of truth (e.g. in mathematics) that is contemplated by, but is not the private possession of, the individual human mind. He chooses rather to start with a notion more familiar to ordinary believers in God—that God made the world and keeps it going; and he tries to show that God exists by arguments of the form: since the world is of such-and-such a nature, there must be some being who made it and keeps it going; we give this being the name 'God'.

The name 'God' thus introduced is regarded by Aquinas, not as a proper name, but as a general term (*nomen naturae*) so far as its mode of significance goes. There is indeed, he holds, only one God; but *there being many Gods* would be not an untrue supposition but merely unintelligible, if what were in question were the plurality of a given named individual. Aquinas rejects the idea that 'God' is necessarily used equivocally by polytheists and by monotheists: he holds that the polytheist *may* be using the word 'God' in the same sense when he says his idol is God, as the missionary when he says that the idol is not God but a senseless block. (In a work of Hindu propaganda I have seen it explained that by priestly consecration of

* P. T. Geach's commentary on Aquinas from *Three Philosophers,* edited by G. E. M. Anscombe and P. T. Geach (Oxford, 1961). Reprinted by permission of the publishers, Basil Blackwell & Mott, Ltd.

an idol the Infinite becomes circumscribed, the Living One a lifeless block, the Omniscient insensible—such is the Divine condescension!) A strong point in favour of Aquinas's view is that 'God' is *translated* into other languages, not *transliterated* as proper names are.

Though the word 'God' is introduced to refer to the Maker and Sustainer of the world, that is not its definition. The term 'helium' was first introduced to refer to an element that produced a certain line in the solar spectrum; but 'source of such-and-such a line in the solar spectrum' was not the definition of the term 'helium'; 'helium' was introduced as a new term in the category of 'nouns of material', like 'hydrogen' and 'gold', to refer to a material known only by inference not by examination of samples. Similarly, 'God' refers to the type of life that would belong to the Maker and Sustainer of the world, rather than to the acts of making and sustaining the world; and so, when the spiritual writers say that man may by grace 'become God', they mean that man may come to share in the special type of life that belongs to God, not that he may come to share in God's creative and sustaining activity.

These remarks on what mode of signification the term 'God' has do not make it the less true that to *prove* there is a God would be to *prove* that somebody made everything else, in the relevant sense of the verb 'made'. But what is the relevant sense, and how can it be learned and taught? Aquinas would say we learned it by analogy with other senses of 'making'; there are various familiar senses of the word, with complex likenesses and differences between them, and we may show how the word is applied to God by bringing out the likenesses and differences between this use and the familiar uses.

For example, in one respect the use of the word when applied to God is more like 'the minstrel made music' than 'the blacksmith made a shoe'; for the shoe is made out of pre-existing material, and, once made, goes on existing independently of the smith; whereas the minstrel did not make the music out of pre-existing sounds, and the music stops if he stops making it; and similarly God did not make the world out of anything pre-existing, and its continued existence depends upon his activity.

It might be objected that it would be impracticable to specify all the necessary modifications of the concept *making* at the outset; yet without this we do not know what we have proved in proving that somebody *made* the world. But Aquinas would hold that the modifications need not be specified at the outset, but will be brought out dialectically from the fact that what is said to be made is the world. For instance, the world cannot have been made out of pre-existing material; for that material would itself already have been *in* the world. Again, though there is no making without change in that which is made, the making of the world would have to be without change occurring in the Maker, and in this respect unlike all other examples of making; for a Maker who was undergoing change because of making things would just be one of that system of interrelated changing things which we call the world, and so *not* the Maker of the world.

Again, someone may say that when all the requisite modifications of the old senses of 'made' have been carried out, we are left not with a new, theological sense of the word but with an empty word whose sense has evaporated. Such evaporation of sense is a real danger with transferred uses of words. But we clearly could not take seriously a general objection to transferred uses of words; nor can the present objection be used to bar theological discussion at the very outset—though perhaps it might turn out that someone who had let himself follow theological discussion up to a point, for the sake of argument, found himself in a position to say: Surely by this series of qualifications you have destroyed the sense of the word 'made' altogether.

I have spoken of God as the Maker of *the world*. This notion, as we shall see, raises problems; some theologians would wish to avoid them by proving God's existence from the existence of some casually chosen thing, not from the existence of the world, and might argue that in spite of using the term 'world' (*mundus*) Aquinas's real mind was like theirs on this point. I think they are wrong as to the feasibility of such a proof, and it is fairly easy to show that Aquinas would not have agreed with them. If we ask an ordinary causal question about a particular thing, the answer need not be 'God': the cause of a man's existence, say, is that he was generated by his parents. 'But couldn't we ask the same question about them?' Certainly: but the possibility of asking a new question in no way implies that the original question was unsatisfactorily asked. 'But if a man had parents and they had parents and so on back *ad infinitum*, wouldn't this regress be vicious?' Not at all. If the meaning of the original answer 'John was generated by his parents' depended on our ability to say who *their* parents were, then the supposition of a chain of ancestors going back *ad infinitum* would involve the absurdity that we could not understand the original answer without completing the whole infinite series of answers. But on the contrary the original answer is understandable without raising the question of grand-parents.

Aquinas accordingly holds that God cannot be reached by saying that this sort of causal chain must end in him: the chain could be endless. He uses the simile of an immortal blacksmith who has been making horseshoes from all eternity, and has naturally worn out no end of hammers in the process: the making of the horseshoe now on the anvil depends only upon the smith as efficient cause and the hammer currently in use as instrument; and though no end of hammers have in fact been broken in the past, they have nothing to do with the case. Similarly, God uses parents to produce a new human being: since they are mortal, he does not use the same pair of parents each time; but as regards understanding the production of this human being here and now, we need not bring into account all the past and perished generations of men, and it is no matter whether they were a finite or infinite series.

Just as the blacksmith, the hammer, and the horseshoe are related in the same way each time, so God's action is involved, according to Aquinas, in the same way for the production of each new generation of men, and each set of parents are alike 'second causes' used instrumentally by the First Cause. The view that the backward series of generations logically has to be finite and terminate in God would on the contrary involve that in generating the first set of parents were causally closer to God than any subsequent parents: a strange result, which would surely be unwelcome to some proponents of the view.

It seems clear, then, that in spite of what a hasty reading of Aquinas's 'Five Ways' might suggest, he did not think God could be reached by following to its end a causal chain starting from a random object. I shall argue that what is in fact essential to the 'Five Ways' is something tantamount to treating the world as a great big object. (It is after all natural to us so to regard the world—'Heaven and Earth', as it is called in the Old Testament—as the upper limit of the series: Earth, solar system, galaxy, cluster of galaxies, . . .) If the world is an object, it again seems natural to ask about it the sort of causal questions which would be legitimate about its parts. If it began to exist, what brought it into existence? In any case, what keeps it from perishing, as some of its parts perish? And what keeps its processes going? And to what end?

The question now arises whether there is any relevant difference if we are considering the world as a whole. Now of course someone might argue, in the style of Kant's antinomies, that we get into intractable problems if we use 'the world' as a subject of predicates—e.g. as to the world's being spatially or temporally finite or infinite. Aquinas was not unaware of such problems, but did not think them intractable: he thought e.g. that the world might or might not have had an infinite past duration, and that neither alternative led to contradiction. What would have appeared to him not worth discussion at all is the idea that, though we can speak without contradiction of the world as a whole, we cannot raise concerning it the sort of causal questions that we can raise concerning its parts. Why should we not raise them? It would be childish to say the world is too big for such questions to be reasonable; and to say the world is all-inclusive would be to beg the question— God would not be included in the world.

Further, Aquinas would not be embarrassed by the question: If it is reasonable to ask who made the world, then why is it not reasonable to ask who made God? For the world shares with its parts certain attributes that give rise to causal questions: it is a complex whole of parts and is in process of change. But, Aquinas would say, God is not a whole of parts and is unchangeable; so the same causal questions need not arise about him. Moreover, precisely because we should soon find ourselves in difficulties if we raised questions about the whole consisting of the world *plus* God—e.g. whether it is caused or uncaused, changeable or unchangeable—Aquinas would deny the legitimacy of speaking of such a whole.

If we now consider the 'five ways' in detail, we shall see that four of them quite clearly depend on the legitimacy of that lumping-together of things by which one would pass from particular things to the world as a whole. The first two 'ways' differ only in that one relates to processes of change and the other to things' coming to be; the further argument is quite parallel in each case. If B is the cause of a process going on in A, or of A's coming to be, then it may be that this happens because of a process in B that is caused by a further thing C; and C in turn may act because of a process in C caused by D; and so on. But now let us lump together the chain of things B, C, D, . . . , and call it X. We may predicate of each one of the causes B, C, D, . . . , *and also* of X as a whole, that it causes a process in A (or the coming-to-be of A) in virtue of being *itself* in process of change. But what is it that maintains this process of change in X? Something that cannot itself be in process of change: for if it were, it would just be one of the things in process of change that causes the process in A (or the coming-to-be of A); i.e. it would after all be just part of the changeable system of causes we called X, and not the cause of the process in X. Thus we are led to a change-less cause of the change and coming-to-be in the world: following Aristotle, Aquinas finds an adumbration of this is Anaxagoras, whose *Nous* was pervasive of the world without being mixed up with its materials or changed by its changes and on that very account had control over the world. The number of terms in X is irrelevant; and the changeless cause is introduced as the cause of the change in the whole system X, not as the last link in a chain, directly related only to the last link but one.

The third 'way' deals with contingent and necessary existence (Aquinas's actual word is '*possibilia*', not '*contingentia*'; but this does not signify). To understand this proof properly, we must first of all see the total mistake of trying here to construe contingency and necessity *à la* Leibniz, in terms of its being contingently or necessarily true that there is a so-and-so. This is a double misconstruction. First, 'there being' a so-and-so is not, as we saw, what Aquinas means by *esse*; and only this will turn out relevant to the proof. Secondly, the necessity or contingency that is here in question is not the *logical* necessity or contingency of some (existential) statement. Accordingly, the attacks on the notion of a logically necessary existential statement simply do not touch the third 'way' at all.

It may be objected that there is simply no sense to the word 'necessary', or none that can be coherently explained, apart from the logical necessity of statements. This thesis is upheld with great confidence in some recent essays on 'philosophical theology'; one author actually says concerning it: 'I have no space to demonstrate this here, and indeed I do not think that it is any longer in need of demonstration'. It may well be wondered how much study of modal logic—

whether, indeed, any knowledge of there being such a discipline—lies at the bottom of such confidence. Anyhow, since what is 'necessary' is what 'cannot' not be, to say that 'necessary' can only refer to logical necessity is equivalent to saying that whatever cannot be so, *logically* cannot be so—e.g. that since I cannot speak Russian, my speaking Russian is logically impossible: which is absurd.

The true interpretation of the third 'way' may be seen e.g. from the parallel passage in the *Contra Gentes*; contingency of existence is established, not from I know not what 'sense' or 'experience' of contingency, but from the plain fact that some things are perishable; and again, the 'necessity' that is asserted of God is identified in Aristotelian style with eternity —with imperishable existence that has no liability to cease. With this clue, we may read the third 'way' as follows: Some things are genuinely liable to cease existing. But not every thing can be of this character: for then, Aquinas tacitly assumes, a universe entirely composed of perishable things would itself be perishable. (At this step there comes in the 'lumping together' previously discussed.) Now such a universe cannot have always existed; Aquinas finds it impossible that a universe with a genuine liability to perish, and without anything outside it to stop it perishing, should have existed an unlimited time without perishing. So, if such a universe is all that exists, then once upon a time nothing at all existed; but in that case nothing would exist now, which is absurd. 'Contingent', i.e. perishable, beings thus cannot exist alone: there must also be at least one 'necessary', i.e. imperishable, being. It is irrelevant to object to this proof that a material universe wholly composed of corruptible things might go on existing even if all its parts actually corrupted, because their matter could still exist under different forms; for the objection presupposes that this matter is not perishable as such, in the way that the things composed of it are; but then this matter will itself be one of the imperishable things Aquinas is talking about at this stage of the proof.

So far, then, what Aquinas claims to have shown is that the class of 'necessary' existents is not empty. He does not go on to argue that this class has only one member, namely God; nor did he believe this. Apart from the imperishable matter of things, spirits and human souls are 'necessary', in that they have no inherent liability to stop existing—*potentia ad non esse*; for they have no matter in their make-up that could assume a different form, or split up into many pieces, or (as people have sometimes fancied) be merged in a larger whole. What Aquinas does argue is that 'necessary', i.e. imperishable, things are imperishable either of themselves or derivatively; now there cannot be an endless series of things deriving imperishability each from its successor; therefore there must be a thing which not only is 'necessary' or imperishable, but is so underivatively or in its own right: and this is God. As regards the 'infinite series' part of this argument, he refers back to the second 'way'; accordingly, if I have rightly interpreted the second 'way', what is being argued there is as follows: A series of only-derivatively-imperishable things may be 'lumped together', and thus considered will form a system which is in its turn only-derivatively-imperishable; that, then, from which the system derives its imperishable character cannot form part of the system, and cannot occur in the series at any point, but rather each term of the series will owe its imperishable character to something outside the series.

The statement of the fourth 'way' in the *Summa Theologica* is odd and obscure to a modern reader; it involves *inter alia* an odd notion of degrees of truth—not *à la* Bradley, but apparently on the score that if one lie is a bigger lie than another, the truth opposed to one is a bigger truth than the truth opposed to the other. I can make no use of this idea, and will rather show how Aquinas might argue from the degrees of *esse* and of goodness, which also he here alludes to; I am not confident that this gives an historically correct exposition of the fourth 'way' (a proof which I sometimes suspect of being one of the indefensible remnants of Platonism in Aquinas's thought); but at least the argument I shall give can be paralleled in many parts of Aquinas's writings (e.g. in Ia q. 4 art. 2).

As we saw when we were deploying the arguments for a real distinction between a form and the corresponding *esse*, if any perfection occurs in a thing only to a degree, this requires a real distinction between the individual instance of the perfection and the degree to which that perfection is found. Now such occurrence of a perfection, Aquinas holds, requires a cause; for the fact that the perfection occurs gives no reason why it occurs only to such a degree and no more; so what accounts for the actual degree to which the perfection occurs—i.e., on Aquinas's view, accounts for the *esse* of that perfection—must be something outside the thing that has the perfection to that limited degree. The only source of perfections with regard to which such a problem would not again arise would have to be some thing possessing perfections not to a degree but without limit—God, who is 'infinite in all perfections' as the Penny Catechism says.

There is an apparent lacuna in this proof; the transition *from* a perfection's being derivative *to* its being derived from a being whose perfections are underivative has not been justified. But it would be easy to construct here an argument parallel to those used in the other three 'ways'. Alternatively, one might treat the fourth 'way', not as a new proof that there is a God, but as telling us something further about God— that the source of all process in the world, and of all beings in it, 'necessary' or 'contingent', is also the source of all perfections in the world, and possesses every perfection illimitably.

The fifth 'way' uses that notion of 'tendencies' which I have expounded. Aquinas argues that the process of the world as a whole (*omnia*) is goal-directed like the arrow shot by an archer, and must therefore owe its direction to the Cause of the world. Aquinas is not here appealing to empirical evidence of detailed 'adaptations'. His starting-point is the existence of a single cosmic order; and some such assumption is continually made in modern science, when (let us say) experiments in a terrestrial laboratory and observations of an explosion in a distant nebula are treated as mutually relevant. Now causal order, on Aquinas's view, is describable only in terms of fulfilment of tendency; and if there is a Cause of the world, the cosmic tendencies will proceed from that Cause. Further Aquinas holds that, though a tendency need not be conscious, unconscious tendency is always derivative: unless the idea or consideration (*ratio*) of an end, and of an operation's being directed towards the end, is found in an agent, the agent's tendency towards the end, though it may be genuinely inherent in the agent and conformable to the agent's nature, will be a derivative tendency. So, Aquinas argues, the unconscious cosmic tendency is derivative, and presupposes an Agent outside the natural order who has thought and design.

Having thus established the existence of a God who is the cause of the world and of the processes in it, Aquinas discusses what we can say about God. We are at once arrested by his saying that as regards God we cannot answer the question '*quid est*?': if we cannot say what God is, what is the use of going on? This puzzle arises only from our forgetting the restricted sense of the Latin, as compared with the English, question. As I said, the word 'God' refers to the type of life enjoyed by the Maker of the World; this is a type of life not to be found by observations *within* the world, like the life enjoyed by men or cats or cabbages, and this hiddenness of the life signified by the word 'God' is expressed by Aquinas's denial that we know concerning God *quid est*. Aquinas is not saying that we cannot make true predications concerning God.

A problem now arises that would justifiably worry people with a modern logical training: how are we to construe the various predications concerning God that Aquinas seeks to establish *before*, and as a means to, establishing the proposition that there is only one God? Since for Aquinas 'God' is not a proper name but a general term, we surely need to settle whether 'God is X' means 'any God (any being that is a God) is X', or 'some God is X', or 'the (one and only) God is X'; we might suspect that Aquinas failed to specify this because Latin so unfortunately lacks articles. But though Aquinas omits to answer the question in advance, there is I think evidence that he would have regarded such statements of natural theology as not being of any of these types, but as being of the unquantifiable type illustrated by 'man is an animal' and 'man is a machine': the predicates (if truly predicated) attach to the subject in virtue of the nature *being a God* that this term signifies. Once it has been proved that there is only one God, any one of these statements may be reconstrued as holding true of the one and only God.

A few remarks here on the logic of 'there is but one God' and 'the one and only God'. On Russell's theory of descriptions, 'the one and only God is X' would be construed as meaning:

'For some y, y is God, and, for any z, if z is God, z is the same as y, and y is X';

and this, shorn of the final clause 'and y is X', would also give the analysis of 'there is but one God'. Aquinas would certainly have objected, on general grounds, to the clause 'z is the same as y'; the sameness, as we saw, must for him be specified by some general term signifying a form or nature. Now the general term that we need to supply here is clearly 'God'; so 'there is but one God' will come out as:

'For some y, y is God, and, for any z, if z is God, z is the same God as y'.

It is important to notice that this would leave open the possibility of there being several Divine Persons; there would still be but one God, if we could truly say that any Divine Person was the same God as any other Divine Person. Now different Persons' being the same God is not manifestly impossible: for, in general, x and y may be the same F although different things are true of x and of y. On the other hand, since all the propositions of natural theology tell us only what is true of a being in virtue of his being God, they cannot serve to establish any distinction there might be between two Persons both of whom were God and the same God. Thus, so far as natural theology goes, the question whether many distinct Persons can be one and the same God is *demonstrably undecidable*, on Aquinas's view; this notion of something's being demonstrably undecidable within a given theory is one that recent logical research has made familiar and unexceptionable. As we shall see, Aquinas held there was a whole class of such questions. In this instance, he held it important not to prove God's unity in such a sense as to rule out the possibility of a Trinity; for certain 'monotheistic' expressions are to be rejected as false by Christian believers—God is not to be spoken of as *sole, singular, unique,* or *solitary* (Ia q. 31 art. 3, 4).

When 'there is but one God' is put into the mis-leading form 'God is One', the numeral 'one' is taken to express an important Divine attribute—and curi-ously strong emotions are aroused, as is hinted by the initial capital. Aquinas wished to remove this august character from the word 'one'; the use of 'one' in speaking about God (and of other numerals, e.g. 'three'—and 'five'—in Trinitarian theology) does not correspond to any Divine attribute whatsoever; noth-ing that is affirmatively predicable of God (*ponitur in divinis*) is expressed by a numerical term. 'One' never in any case expresses an attribute of things, ex-cept when the word is taken in the 'discrete-quantity' meaning of *being all in one piece*, which is not ap-plicable to God; all that 'there is *one* God' signifies over and above 'there is (a) God' is *indivisio*—that it is *not* the case, for any x and y, that x is a *different* God from y.

Now how does Aquinas think this can be proved? There are two sorts of difference that there might be between two different animals in a zoo: material difference, between two individuals of the same kind, and formal difference, between individuals of different kinds. If a God is necessarily immaterial, then there cannot be material difference between two Gods; and Aquinas argues that a God must be immaterial, because God is the unchanging cause of change, whereas any body causes change only in that it simultaneously undergoes change (*nullum corpus movet non motum*). Just as Anaxagoras said that Mind must be 'unmixed' with the material world in order to know and rule it, so Aquinas holds that the unchanging cause of all the changes in the physical world must itself be non-physical. Material multiplication of Gods is thus impossible. Further, the fourth 'way' established that a God is infinite in all perfections; but if there were diverse Deities, one would excel in one perfection (say, justice) and another in another (say, mercy); so there cannot be a formal multiplication of Gods either, as the heathen have fancied. There remains indeed the possibility that two or more Persons, while equally unlimited in all perfections, should be distinct in virtue of some asymmetrical relation or relations holding between them. But any such Persons would be one and the same God; we must not be misled by a false imagination of the material difference that makes two human persons to be different men.

In the sequel, then, we may justifiably speak of proving the attributes of *God*; the question which

God, or which Divine Person, we are talking about, will never arise.

Since God is immaterial, it follows at once on Aquinas's doctrine of thought that he is a living self-subsistent thought of himself. But God is not, as Aristotle allegedly believed, the only object of his own thought. If God is a self-subsistent thought, his causality of the world can only be that sort of causality in which what comes to be outside the agent is a fulfilment of a tendency proceeding from the agent's consideration; and this, as we saw, is Aquinas's account of *voluntary* causality. God, then, is the cause of the world in that he envisages such a world and chooses that it should be. Here Aquinas's doctrine stands in noteworthy contrast with that of Spinoza, whose arguments are often paralleled in his most seriously considered objections.

Aquinas is insistent that God's creation of the world is absolutely free. He rejects the idea that God was bound to desire the best of all possible worlds; because there is no sense in talking of a best possible world, any more than of a biggest possible number. And still less can the creation of a world that is less good than another possible world be overwhelmingly attractive to the Divine Nature which already enjoys all perfections without measure—*ipsa suis pollens opibus, nil indiga nostri*. Moreover, God can be under no obligation to create anything: to whom could he owe it? In all God's works there is 'mercy' and 'justice': but the 'mercy' whereby God gratuitously, without need or obligation, brings a creature into existence is more fundamental than the 'justice' whereby he gives it what befits its nature.

We should notice that Aquinas's ascription of thought and will to God essentially derives from his account of the concepts *thought* and *will*. If these concepts were got from a particular experience, whether quasi-sensory or not, there would be no more ground for ascribing thought and will to God than for ascribing to him the passions we feel or even the colours we see. But Aquinas holds that a thought is in a way thought of just in virtue of one's having that thought, and needs no special added experience to bring it to the mind's ken; and that our reflection on the distinctive feature of thought shows this to be, not a recognisable quality like anger or redness, but a manner of *esse*, which accordingly there is nothing to hinder our ascribing to God even though we have no concrete knowledge of the Divine Life.

The false doctrine of will that we discussed under the heading *Operations and Tendencies* would lead to the supposition that the coming-to-be of the world was (at least logically) posterior to God's enacting within himself a 'volition' or 'decree' to create the world; many intractable problems have arisen about this supposed 'volition'. I have argued that, even as regards human voluntary actions, voluntariness consists for Aquinas in proceeding from the agent in a special manner, not in being the effect of something called a volition; certainly his proof that the world proceeds from God's will introduces no such intermediary entity as a creative 'volition', but simply argues that God's mode of causality must be voluntary causality and not natural causality.

No question as to what God does in fact will to exist is soluble by natural theology; where free choice exists, no logic will enable us to deduce what is in fact chosen. (If, for instance, as Aquinas thought, a world with a beginning in time and one without a beginning are alike logically possible, natural theology cannot tell

us which sort of world ours is.) There are thus an
enormous number of questions that natural theology
cannot answer; and no place for the presumptuous
dream of Socrates in the *Phaedo*, that we could deduce
what the world is like from our fancies of how it ought
to be.

Before going further, we must expound Aquinas's
doctrine of the Divine 'simplicity'.

It is part of the religious tradition to which Aquinas
belongs to use abstract terms as well as concrete ones
in designating God: to say that he is Wisdom, Power,
and Love, not only wise, powerful and loving. One way
of explaining this might be to say in Hobbes's style
that the word we use for God 'ought to signify our
desire to honour him with the best appellations we
can think on', and that these abstract words are mere
'attributes of honour'; and this would be supported by
the interesting fact that just such abstract expressions
do express special honour or devotion among men—a
lover praises his mistress by saying 'you are sweetness itself' rather than 'you are sweet', and an ec-
clesiastic is addressed more ceremoniously as 'your
Paternity' than as 'Father'. One Praepositivus is mentioned by Aquinas as favouring this sort of account.

The generality of theologians, however, held that
this use of abstract terms concerning God was not a
mere honorific way of speaking, but must be taken
seriously as expressing a real difference between God
and creatures. Aquinas's doctrine concerning *quod*
and *quo*, which I expounded in connexion with forms,
is powerfully applied here: what is meant by 'God is
Wisdom', he holds, is that the terms 'God' and 'the
wisdom of God' are both ways of referring to one and
the same reality; and likewise 'the power of God'
again refers to the same reality. The attributes re-

ferred to by 'the wisdom of—' and 'the power of—' are indeed different, but the wisdom of God and the power of God are identical (cf. Ia q. 32 art. 3 ad 3 um).

The difficulty here is to exclude from one's mind the Platonism that Aquinas combats—the 'barbarous' misconstruction of 'the wisdom of God' as 'wisdom, which belongs to, is a property of, God'; if we do think on these lines, Aquinas will appear to be saying that wisdom and power are different, but God possesses both, and in him they are not different but identical—which is sheer self-contradiction. The analogy of mathematical functions, which I used before, proves valuable here too. 'The square of—' and 'the double of—' signify two quite different functions, but for the argument 2 these two functions both take the number 4 as their value. Similarly, 'the wisdom of—' and 'the power of—' signify different forms, but the individualizations of these forms in God's case are not distinct from one another; nor is either distinct from God, just as the number 1 is in no way distinct from its own square. And again, 'the *esse* of God', 'that by which God *is*', signifies nothing distinct from Him-who-is.

It is a very short way from these considerations to the severe difficulties of the view that discourse concerning God is 'analogical'. It would be better to say that it turns out to be analogical: what happens, on Aquinas's view, is that we first call God 'wise'; then discover that 'the wisdom of God' is a designation of God himself, whereas the like does not hold of any other being whom we rightly call 'wise'; and thus reflecting upon this, we see that 'wise' cannot be applied to God in the same way as to other beings. The difficulty is to show that this conclusion is not a mere *reductio ad absurdum:* starting from the premise that God can be called 'wise', we reach the conclusion that he cannot in the ordinary sense be so called, which surely contradicts the premise.

An attempt has been made to remove the difficulty by appealing to 'proportionality': God's wisdom, to be sure, is entirely different from man's, but God's wisdom is to God as man's wisdom is to man. This is, of course, a mathematical metaphor—'x is to a as b is to c; required to find x'—and it is a thoroughly bad one. A rule-of-three sum can be worked only if three of the quantities involved are known; but God is not 'known' in the relevant sense—i.e. something encountered as an item in the world. (As I explained in discussing *esse*, knowing *that there is* a God is a very different matter.) Moreover, since God's wisdom is supposedly identical with God, but not man's wisdom with man, the metaphor breaks down at once: for we cannot have in mathematics that x is to a as b is to c, and $x = a$, but not $b = c$.

Our own mathematical metaphor of functions does something to lessen these difficulties. We can produce an actual example of a number that is its own square and its own cube, namely the number 1; but there may very well be functions, say F ( ) and G ( ), such that we can prove the mathematical theorem that, for some x or other, $x = F (x) = G (x)$, without being able to cite a particular number satisfying this equation; we may even be able to prove that any number which did satisfy the equation would be too large to be distinctly apprehended. And this is like what Aquinas is maintaining about God: that we can know which attributes are meant by general terms like 'wise' and 'just', and also *know that* there is a being, whom we call 'God', whose wisdom and justice and *esse* are identical with him and with one another; even though we *have no insight into* the simple nature that verifies all these predicates simultaneously, without room for a distinction between *quod* and *quo*, between the individual occurrence of attributes and the God in whom they occur, or between God and his *esse*.

There is, then, no obvious incoherence in the doctrine that God is his own Nature, his own attributes, his own *esse*. But how is this doctrine proved? and what are its consequences?

The fourth 'way' as I interpret it (an interpretation certainly conformable to what Aquinas says elsewhere) is in essentials the argument that what possesses a perfection only to a degree does not possess it underivatively. God's perfections are illimitable because there is in no case a distinction between the perfection he has and the degree to which he has it, as there would be if it were possible for him to have that very perfection to a higher degree; and where such a distinction does exist, a perfection is necessarily derivative. Now for Aquinas the degree to which a perfection is possessed must be regarded as the *esse* of that instance of the perfection. We may thus naturally pass to a generalised form of the argument. If there is ever a distinction between an individualised form or nature and the corresponding *esse*, then the *esse* of that form or nature must be caused; an individualised form or nature that is not its own *esse* cannot have *esse* in its own right. God, then, must be his own *esse*; otherwise there would be a cause that supplied *esse* to the Divine Nature, which is absurd. And each Divine perfection is identical with its own *esse*, and thus with God.

From this doctrine of God's 'simplicity', it follows

that God is unchangeable and eternal. Of any change-able thing x, we have to say that it remains the same F while changing from G to not-G or *vice versa*; but if God changed from being G to being not-G or *vice versa* while remaining the same God, we should have to assert a real distinction between his G-ness and his possession of the Divine Nature, which we cannot do. So God is in every respect unchangeable. Eternity is defined by Aquinas (following Boethius) as the simul-taneous and complete possession of unending life; be-ing unchangeable, God is eternal.

We must not conceive of God's eternity as like the timelessness of mathematics: the primeness of the number 7 simply has no relation to dates, whereas God's eternity is compresent with every part of time; so we can properly say 'God existed yesterday', 'God sees to-day what men do', whereas '7 was prime yesterday' is nonsensical. Aquinas even holds that different predicates are true of God at different times; if Socrates first sits down and then gets up, then we must say of God first that he knows that Socrates is sitting and then that he knows that Socrates is stand-ing. How this is possible without a change within God's mind Aquinas does not try to say; the way an eternal mind operates is naturally not fully under-standable by us. (Ia q. 14 art. 15 ad 3 um.)

Let us then sum up Aquinas's teaching as to man's natural knowledge of God. In an inchoate form, this knowledge is available to all men who are sufficiently reflective to think of the world-order as a whole and wonder how it came to be and how it is sustained; and most men have believed in its governance by superior power to which they gave the name God. But just as men who can tell living from non-living things may give the most grotesque account of what it is to have life or soul (e.g. that the soul is a small or rarefied man), so men who recognise that there is a God ruling the world may give grotesque accounts of him (e.g. that he is an immortal and powerful man). There is no innate idea of God by appeal to which such follies are refutable.

Natural theology can show us some of the main attributes of God, and expose some of the grosser errors about him. But a serious study of natural theology requires a rigorous philosophical training, for which few have leisure, talents, or inclination. Moreover, the divergent views of great philosophers who have pursued this study show that there is still risk of grave error.

What is more, the God of whom natural theology apprises us is frightening: we depend for our very existence from moment to moment on a Being of infinite knowledge and power, whose will in our regard we know in advance to be beyond our skills of calculation. It is just as well that we should be frightened: the fear of the Lord is the beginning of wisdom. But if wisdom were not more than this, we might well despair, thinking of man as he is; what if God should will that this miserably wicked race should utterly destroy itself?

For Aquinas, however, the wisdom of natural theology is only the beginning: our puzzles are replaced by certainties, and our fear by hope, because of the relevation God has freely given through Jesus Christ.

> Sinners be glad, and penance do,
>   And thank your Maker heartfully;
> For he that ye might not come to
>   To you is comen full humbly

Your soulis with his blood to buy
And loose you of the fiend's arrest,
And only of his own mercy;
Pro nobis Puer natus est.

B. THE CLASSICAL CRITIQUE

1. DAVID HUME (1711–76)

[David Hume's *Dialogues Concerning Natural Religion* is rightly one of the most celebrated contributions to philosophical theology in Western thought. The book is small, but its thesis is forcefully drawn. In dialogue is a cast of three characters, each of whom represents a common attitude about God. *Demea* is a metaphysical theist whose arguments stand or fall on certain *a priori* notions about evidence. *Cleanthes* is an anthropomorphic theist who argues from the fact of the world to the necessity of a divine source. And *Philo* is clearly Hume as skeptic. In the selection that follows, both Cleanthes and Philo attack the rationalism of Demea. Cleanthes argues that matters of fact cannot be demonstrated by the mere introduction of *a priori* assertions. "No assertion is demonstrable unless its contrary implies a contradiction." Philo, while agreeing with Cleanthes, sees yet another difficulty. Demea has assumed that rational necessity entails a divine mind; but, on the contrary, it may be only a manifestation of the absolute natural character of the universe.]

Critique of the Cosmological Argument*

But if so many difficulties attend the argument à *posteriori*, said Demea, had we not better adhere to

---

* From *Dialogues Concerning Natural Religion*, Part IX. *The Philosophical Works of David Hume* (Boston, 1854).

that simple and sublime argument *à priori,* which, by offering to us infallible demonstration, cuts off at once all doubt and difficulty? By this argument, too, we may prove the INFINITY of the Divine attributes, which, I am afraid, can never be ascertained with certainty from any other topic. For how can an effect, which either is finite, or, for aught we know, may be so; how can such an effect, I say, prove an infinite cause? The unity too of the Divine Nature, it is very difficult, if not absolutely impossible, to deduce merely from contemplating the works of nature; nor will the uniformity alone of the plan, even were it allowed, give us any assurance of that attribute. Whereas the argument *à priori* . . .

You seem to reason, Demea, interposed Cleanthes, as if those advantages and conveniences in the abstract argument were full proofs of its solidity. But it is first proper, in my opinion, to determine what argument of this nature you choose to insist on; and we shall afterwards, from itself, better than from its *useful* consequences, endeavor to determine what value we ought to put upon it.

The argument, replied Demea, which I would insist on, is the common one. Whatever exists must have a cause or reason of its existence; it being absolutely impossible for any thing to produce itself, or be the cause of its own existence. In mounting up, therefore, from effects to causes, we must either go on in tracing an infinite succession, without any ultimate cause at all; or must at last have recourse to some ultimate cause, that is *necessarily* existent: now, that the first supposition is absurd, may be thus proved. In the infinite chain or succession of causes and effects, each single effect is determined to exist by the power and efficacy of that cause which immediately preceded;

but the whole external chain or succession, taken together, is not determined or caused by any thing; and yet it is evident that it requires a cause or reason, as much as any particular object which begins to exist in time. The question is still reasonable, why this particular succession of causes existed from eternity, and not any other succession, or no succession at all. If there be no necessarily existent being, any supposition which can be formed is equally possible; nor is there any more absurdity in Nothing's having existed from eternity, than there is in that succession of causes which constitutes the universe. What was it, then, which determined Something to exist rather than Nothing, and bestowed being on a particular possibility, exclusive of the rest? *External causes,* there are supposed to be none. *Chance* is a word without a meaning. Was it *Nothing?* But that can never produce any thing. We must, therefore, have recourse to a necessarily existent Being, who carries the REASON of his existence in himself, and who cannot be supposed not to exist, without an express contradiction. There is, consequently, such a Being; that is, there is a Deity.

I shall not leave it to Philo, said Cleanthes, though I know that the starting objections is his chief delight, to point out the weakness of this metaphysical reasoning. It seems to me so obviously ill-grounded, and at the same time of so little consequence to the cause of true piety and religion, that I shall myself venture to show the fallacy of it.

I shall begin with observing, that there is an evident absurdity in pretending to demonstrate a matter of fact, or to prove it by any arguments *à priori.* Nothing is demonstrable, unless the contrary implies a contradiction. Nothing, that is distinctly conceivable, implies a contradiction. Whatever we conceive as existent, we can also conceive as non-existent. There is no being, therefore, whose non-existence implies a contradiction. Consequently there is no being, whose existence is demonstrable. I propose this argument as entirely decisive, and am willing to rest the whole controversy upon it.

It is pretended that the Deity is a necessarily existent being; and this necessity of his existence is attempted to be explained by asserting, that if we knew his whole essence or nature, we should perceive it to be as impossible for him not to exist, as for twice two not to be four. But it is evident that this can never happen, while our faculties remain the same as at present. It will still be possible for us, at any time, to conceive the non-existence of what we formerly conceived to exist; nor can the mind ever lie under a necessity of supposing any object to remain always in being; in the same manner as we lie under a necessity of always conceiving twice two to be four. The words, therefore, *necessary existence,* have no meaning; or, which is the same thing, none that is consistent.

But further, why may not the material universe be the necessarily existent being, according to this pretended explication of necessity? We dare not affirm that we know all the qualities of matter; and for aught we can determine, it may contain some qualities, which, were they known, would make its non-existence appear as great a contradiction as that twice two is five. I find only one argument employed to prove, that the material world is not the necessarily existent Being: and this argument is derived from the contingency both of the matter and the form of the world. "Any particle of matter," it is said,[1] "may be *con-*

---

[1] Dr. [Samuel] Clarke [1675–1729].

ceived to be annihilated; and any form may be *conceived* to be altered. Such an annihilation or alteration, therefore, is not impossible." But it seems a great partiality not to perceive, that the same argument extends equally to the Deity, so far as we have any conception of him; and that the mind can at least imagine him to be non-existent, or his attributes to be altered. It must be some unknown, inconceivable qualities, which can make his non-existence appear impossible, or his attributes unalterable: and no reason can be assigned, why these qualities may not belong to matter. As they are altogether unknown and inconceivable, they can never be proved incompatible with it.

Add to this, that in tracing an eternal succession of objects, it seems absurd to inquire for a general cause or first author. How can any thing, that exists from eternity, have a cause, since that relation implies a priority in time, and a beginning of existence?

In such a chain, too, or succession of objects, each part is caused by that which preceded it, and causes that which succeeds it. Where then is the difficulty? But the WHOLE, you say, wants a cause. I answer, that the uniting of these parts into a whole, like the uniting of several distinct countries into one kingdom, or several distinct members into one body, is performed merely by an arbitrary act of the mind, and has no influence on the nature of things. Did I show you the particular causes of each individual in a collection of twenty particles of matter, I should think it very unreasonable, should you afterwards ask me, what was the cause of the whole twenty. This is sufficiently explained in explaining the cause of the parts.

Though the reasonings which you have urged, Cleanthes, may well excuse me, said Philo, from starting any further difficulties, yet I cannot forbear insisting still upon another topic. It is observed by arithmeticians, that the products of 9, compose always either 9, or some lesser product of 9, if you add together all the characters of which any of the former products is composed. Thus, of 18, 27, 36, which are products of 9, you make 9 by adding 1 to 8, 2 to 7, 3 to 6. Thus, 369 is a product also of 9; and if you add 3, 6, and 9, you make 18, a lesser product of 9.[2] To a superficial observer, so wonderful a regularity may be admired as the effect either of chance or design: but a skilful algebraist immediately concludes it to be the work of necessity, and demonstrates, that it must forever result from the nature of these numbers. Is it not probable, I ask, that the whole economy of the universe is conducted by a like necessity, though no human algebra can furnish a key which solves the difficulty? And instead of admiring the order of natural beings, may it not happen, that, could we penetrate into the intimate nature of bodies, we should clearly see why it was absolutely impossible they could ever admit of any other disposition? So dangerous is it to introduce this idea of necessity into the present question! and so naturally does it afford an inference directly opposite to the religious hypothesis!

But dropping all these abstractions, continued Philo, and confining ourselves to more familiar topics, I shall venture to add an observation, that the argument *à priori* has seldom been found very convincing, except to people of a metaphysical head, who have accustomed themselves to abstract reasoning, and who, finding from mathematics, that the under-

[2] *République des Lettres,* Août 1685. *The Philosophical Works of David Hume* (Boston, 1854), Part IX.

standing frequently leads to truth through obscurity, and, contrary to first appearances, have transferred the same habit of thinking to subjects where it ought not to have place. Other people, even of good sense and the best inclined to religion, feel always some deficiency in such arguments, though they are not perhaps able to explain distinctly where it lies; a certain proof that men ever did, and ever will derive their religion from other sources than from this species of reasoning.

2. IMMANUEL KANT (1724–1804)

[The criticism Kant levels in the *Critique of Pure Reason* against the cosmological arguments is commensurate with his earlier rejection of the ontological argument. Although the more familiar form of the ontological argument is St. Anselm's, Kant concentrates on Descartes' version. According to Kant, the Cartesian interpretation begins with the premise that the conception of absolutely necessary Being entails the existence of such a Being. Ostensively, the conception of a non-existent necessary Being is contradictory because a being that is absolutely necessary, but is at the same time non-existent, cannot be so conceived, since it would be contingent and not necessary by virtue of its non-existence. Kant argues that "existence" is not a true predicate, that is, the idea of necessary Being does not logically entail the existence of necessary Being any more than the idea of a griffin entails the existence of a griffin. Moreover, the cosmological arguments begin with the assumption that highest reality, *ens realissimum*, must of necessity include the property existence. But that is merely a transcendental illusion whereby one seeks to extend a notion (here, the definition of Supreme Being) to the realm of existence.]

Of the Impossibility of a Cosmological Proof of the Existence of God*

It was something quite unnatural, and a mere innovation of scholastic wisdom, to attempt to pick out of an entirely arbitrary idea the existence of the object corresponding to it. Such an attempt would never have been made, if there had not existed beforehand a need of our reason of admitting for existence in general something necessary, to which we may ascend and in which we may rest; and if, as that necessity must be unconditioned and *a priori* certain, reason had not been forced to seek a concept which, if possible, should satisfy such a demand and give us a knowledge of an existence entirely *a priori*. Such a concept was supposed to exist in the idea of an *ens realissimum*, and that idea was therefore used for a more definite knowledge of that, the existence of which one had admitted or been persuaded of independently, namely, of the necessary Being. This very natural procedure of reason was carefully concealed, and instead of ending with that concept, an attempt was made to begin with it, and thus to derive from it the necessity of existence, which it was only meant to supplement. Hence arose that unfortunate ontological proof, which satisfies neither the demands of our natural and healthy understanding, nor the requirements of the schools.

The *cosmological proof*, which we have now to examine, retains the connection of absolute necessity

* From *Critique of Pure Reason*, translated by F. Max Müller (New York, 1896).

with the highest reality, but instead of concluding, like the former, from the highest reality necessity in existence, it concludes from the given and unconditioned necessity of any being, its unlimited reality. It thus brings everything at least into the groove of a natural, though I know not whether of a really or only apparently rational syllogism, which carries the greatest conviction, not only for the common, but also for the speculative understanding, and has evidently drawn the first outline of all proofs of natural theology, which have been followed at all times, and will be followed in future also, however much they may be hidden and disguised. We shall now proceed to exhibit and to examine this cosmological proof which Leibniz calls also the proof *a contingentia mundi*.

It runs as follows: If there exists anything, there must exist an absolutely necessary Being also. Now I, at least, exist; therefore there exists an absolutely necessary Being. The minor contains an experience, the major the conclusion from experience in general to the existence of the necessary.[1] This proof therefore begins with experience, and is not entirely *a priori*, or ontological; and, as the object of all possible experience is called the world, this proof is called the *cosmological proof*. As it takes no account of any peculiar property of the objects of experience, by which this world of ours may differ from any other possible world, it is distinguished, in its name also, from the physico-theological proof, which employs as argu-

---

[1] This conclusion is too well known to require detailed exposition. It rests on the apparently transcendental law of causality in nature, that everything *contingent* has its cause, which, if contingent again, must likewise have a cause, till the series of subordinate causes ends in an absolutely necessary cause, without which it could not be complete.

ments, observations of the peculiar property of this our world of sense.

The proof then proceeds as follows: The necessary being can be determined in one way only, that is, by one only of all possible opposite predicates; it must therefore be determined completely by its own concept. There is only one concept of a thing possible, which *a priori*, completely determines it, namely, that of the *ens realissimum*. It follows, therefore, that the concept of the *ens realissimum* is the only one by which a necessary Being can be thought, and therefore it is concluded, that a Highest Being exists by necessity.

There are so many sophistical propositions in this cosmological argument, that it really seems as if speculative reason had spent all her dialectical skill in order to produce the greatest possible transcendental illusion. Before examining it, we shall draw up a list of them, by which reason has put forward an old argument disguised as a new one, in order to appeal to the agreement of two witnesses, one supplied by pure reason, the other by experience, while in reality there is only one, namely, the first, who changes his dress and voice, in order to be taken for a second. In order to have a secure foundation, this proof takes its stand on experience, and pretends to be different from the ontological proof, which places its whole confidence in pure concepts *a priori* only. The cosmological proof, however, uses that experience only in order to make one step, namely, to the existence of a necessary Being in general. What properties that Being may have, can never be learnt from the empirical argument, and for that purpose reason takes leave of it altogether, and tries to find out, from among concepts only, what properties an absolutely necessary Being ought to possess, i.e. which among all possible things contains in itself the requisite conditions (*requisita*) of absolute necessity. This requisite is believed by reason to exist in the concept of an *ens realissimum* only, and reason concludes at once, that this must be the absolutely necessary Being. In this conclusion it is simply assumed that a concept of a being of the highest reality is perfectly adequate to the concept of absolute necessity in existence; so that the former might be concluded from the latter. This is the same proposition as that maintained in the ontological argument, and is simply taken over into the cosmological proof, nay made its foundation, although the intention was to avoid it. It is clear that absolute necessity is an existence from mere concepts. If then I say that the concept of the *ens realissimum* is such a concept, and is the only concept adequate to necessary existence, I am bound to admit that the latter may be deduced from the former. The whole conclusive strength of the so-called cosmological proof rests therefore in reality on the ontological proof from mere concepts, while the appeal to experience is quite superfluous, and, though it may lead us on to the concept of absolute necessity, it cannot demonstrate it with any definite object. For as soon as we intend to do this, we must at once abandon all experience, and try to find out, which among the pure concepts may contain the conditions of the possibility of an absolutely necessary Being. But if in this way the possibility of such a Being has been perceived, its existence also has been proved: for what we are really saying is this, that under all possible things there is one, which carries with it absolute necessity, or that this Being exists with absolute necessity.

Sophisms in arguments are most easily discovered,

if they are put forward in a correct scholastic form. This we shall now proceed to do.

If the proposition is right, that every absolutely necessary Being is, at the same time, the most real Being (and this is the *nervus probandi* of the cosmological proof), it must, like all affirmative judgments, be capable of conversion, at least *per accidens*. This would give us the proposition that some *entia realissima* are at the same time absolutely necessary beings. One *ens realissimum*, however, does not differ from any other on any point, and what applies to one, applies also to all. In this case, therefore, I may employ absolute conversion, and say, that every *ens realissimum* is a necessary being. As this proposition is determined by its concepts *a priori* only, it follows that the mere concept of the *ens realissimum* must carry with it its absolute necessity; and this, which was maintained by the ontological proof, and not recognised by the cosmological, forms really the foundation of the conclusions of the latter, though in a disguised form.

We thus see that the second road, taken by speculative reason, in order to prove the existence of the highest Being, is not only as illusory as the first, but commits in addition an *ignoratio elenchi*, promising to lead us by a new path, but after a short circuit bringing us back to the old one, which we had abandoned for its sake.

I said before, that a whole nest of dialectical assumptions was hidden in that cosmological proof, and that transcendental criticism might easily detect and destroy it. I shall here enumerate them only, leaving it to the experience of the reader to follow up the fallacies and remove them.

We find, first, the transcendental principle of inferring a cause from the accidental. This principle, that everything contingent must have a cause, is valid in the world of sense only, and has not even a meaning outside it. For the purely intellectual concept of the contingent cannot produce a synthetical proposition like that of causality, and the principle of causality has no meaning and no criterion of its use, except in the world of sense, while here it is meant to help us beyond the world of sense.

Secondly. The inference of a first cause, based on the impossibility of an infinite ascending series of given causes in this world of sense,—an inference which the principles of the use of reason do not allow us to draw even in experience, while here we extend that principle beyond experience, whither that series can never be prolonged.

Thirdly. The false self-satisfaction of reason with regard to the completion of that series, brought about by removing in the end every kind of condition, without which nevertheless no concept of necessity is possible, and by then, when any definite concepts have become impossible, accepting this as a completion of our concept.

Fourthly. The mistaking the logical possibility of a concept of all united reality (without any internal contradiction) for the transcendental, which requires a principle for the practicability of such a synthesis, such principle however being applicable to the field of possible experience only, &c.

The trick of the cosmological proof consists only in trying to avoid the proof of the existence of a necessary Being *a priori* by mere concepts. Such a proof would have to be ontological, and of this we feel ourselves quite incapable. For this reason we take a real existence (of any experience whatever), and conclude from it, as well as may be, some absolutely necessary condition of it. In that case there is no necessity for explaining its possibility, because, if it has been proved that it exists, the question as to its possibility is unnecessary. If then we want to determine that necessary Being more accurately, according to its nature, we do not seek what is sufficient to make us understand from its concept the necessity of its existence. If we could do this, no empirical presupposition would be necessary. No, we only seek the negative condition (*conditio sine qua non*), without which a Being would not be absolutely necessary. Now, in every other kind of syllogisms leading from a given effect to its cause, this might well be feasible. In our case, however, it happens unfortunately that the condition which is required for absolute necessity exists in one single Being only, which, therefore, would have to contain in its concept all that is required for absolute necessity, and that renders a conclusion *a priori*, with regard to such necessity, possible. I ought therefore to be able to reason conversely, namely, that everything is absolutely necessary, if that concept (of the highest reality) belongs to it. If I cannot do this (and I must confess that I cannot, if I wish to avoid the ontological proof), I have suffered shipwreck on my new course, and have come back again from where I started. The concept of the highest Being may satisfy all questions *a priori*, which can be asked regarding the internal determinations of a thing, and it is therefore an ideal, without an equal, because the general concept distinguishes it at the same time as an individual being among all possible things. But it does not satisfy the really important question, regarding its own existence; and if some one who admitted the existence of a necessary Being were to ask us, which of all things in the world could be regarded as such, we could not answer: This here is the necessary Being.

It may be allowable to *admit* the existence of a Being entirely sufficient to serve as the cause of all possible effects, simply in order to assist reason in her search for unity of causes. But to go so far as to say that *such a Being exists necessarily,* is no longer the modest language of an admissible hypothesis, but the bold assurance of apodictic certainty; for the knowledge of that which is absolutely necessary must itself possess absolute necessity.

The whole problem of the transcendental Ideal is this, either to find a concept compatible with absolute necessity, or to find the absolute necessity compatible with the concept of anything. If the one is possible, the other must be so also, for reason recognises that only as absolutely necessary which is necessary according to its concept. Both these tasks baffle our attempts at *satisfying* our understanding on this point, and likewise our endeavours to comfort it with regard to its impotence.

That unconditioned necessity, which we require as the last support of all things, is the true abyss of human reason. Eternity itself, however terrible and sublime it may have been depicted by Haller, is far from producing the same giddy impression, for it only *measures* the duration of things, but does not *support* them. We cannot put off the thought, nor can we support it, that a Being, which we represent to ourselves as the highest among all possible beings, should say to himself, I am from eternity to eternity, there is nothing beside me, except that which is something through my will,—*but whence am I?* Here all sinks away from under us, and the highest perfection, like the smallest, passes without support before the eyes of speculative reason, which finds no difficulty in making the one as well as the other to disappear without the slightest impediment.

Many processes of nature, which manifest their existence by certain effects, remain perfectly inscrutable to us, because we cannot follow them up far enough by observation. The transcendental object, which forms the foundation of all phenomena, and with it the ground of our sensibility having this rather than any other supreme conditions, are and always will be inscrutable. The thing no doubt is given, but it is incomprehensible. An ideal of pure reason, however, cannot be called inscrutable, because it cannot produce any credentials of its reality beyond the requirement of reason to perfect all synthetical unity by means of it. As, therefore, it is not even given as an object that can be thought, it cannot be said to be, as such, inscrutable; but, being a mere idea, it must find in the nature of reason its place and its solution, and in that sense be capable of scrutiny. For it is the very essence of reason that we are able to give an account of all our concepts, opinions, and assertions either on objective or, if they are a mere illusion, on subjective grounds.

C. THE CONTEMPORARY REJOINDER

1. PAUL EDWARDS (1923–   )

[Paul Edwards, Professor of Philosophy at Brooklyn College, has long been an exponent of the analytic method in philosophy. In the essay that follows, he applies this method critically to the cosmological arguments. His attention is focused on the causal and contingency forms of the argument. Those who support the notion of a first cause, Edwards argues, rule out the possibility of an infinite series because they confuse an infinite series with one that is merely long. On the other hand, the contingency argument is hardly better off, for it assumes the principle of "necessary being"—a principle that is itself in need of explanation. In other words, any explanation that introduces a special term (or series of terms) without the additional premises necessary for intelligible understanding of these terms is grossly *non sequitur*.]

The Cosmological Argument*

I

The so-called "cosmological proof" is one of the oldest and most popular arguments for the existence

* From *The Rationalist Annual for the Year 1959*, edited by Hector Hawton. Reprinted by permission of Pemburton Publishing Co., Ltd., London.

of God. It was forcibly criticized by Hume,[1] Kant,[2] and Mill,[3] but it would be inaccurate to consider the argument dead or even moribund. Catholic philosophers, with hardly any exception, appear to believe that it is as solid and conclusive as ever. Thus Father F. C. Copleston confidently championed it in his Third Programme debate with Bertrand Russell[4]; and in America, where Catholic writers are more sanguine, we are told by a Jesuit professor of physics that "the existence of an intelligent being as the First Cause of the universe can be established by *rational scientific inference*."[5]

I am absolutely convinced [the same writer continues] that any one who would give the same consideration to that proof (the cosmological argument), as outlined for example in William Brosnan's *God and Reason*, as he would give to a line of argumentation found in the *Physical Review* or the *Proceedings of the Royal Society* would be forced to admit that the cogency of this argument for the existence of God far outstrips that which is found in the reasoning which Chadwick uses to prove the existence of the neutron, which today is accepted as certain as any conclusion in the physical sciences.[6]

Mild theists like the late Professor Dawes Hicks[7] and Dr. [A. C.] Ewing,[8] who concede many of Hume's

[1] *Dialogues Concerning Natural Religion* (London, 1958), Part IX.

[2] *The Critique of Pure Reason*, Transcendental Dialectic, Book II, Chapter III.

[3] "Theism," *Three Essays on Religion*, Part I.

[4] Reprinted in the British edition of Russell's *Why I Am Not a Christian*.

[5] J. S. O'Connor, "A Scientific Approach to Religion," *The Scientific Monthly* (1940), p. 369; my italics.

[6] *Ibid.*, pp. 369–70.

[7] *The Philosophical Bases of Theism*, Lecture V.

[8] *The Fundamental Questions of Philosophy*, Chapter XI.

and Kant's criticisms, nevertheless contend that the argument possesses a certain core of truth. In popular discussions it also crops up again and again—for example, when believers address atheists with such questions as "You tell me where the universe came from!" Even philosophers who reject the cosmological proof sometimes embody certain of its confusions in the formulation of their own position. In the light of all this, it may be worth while to undertake a fresh examination of the argument with special attention to the fallacies that were not emphasized by the older critics.

II

The cosmological proof has taken a number of forms, the most important of which are known as the "causal argument" and "the argument from contingency," respectively. In some writers, in Samuel Clarke for example, they are combined, but it is best to keep them apart as far as possible. The causal argument is the second of the "five ways" of Aquinas and roughly proceeds as follows: we find that the things around us come into being as the result of the activity of other things. These causes are themselves the result of the activity of other things. But such a causal series cannot "go back to infinity." Hence there must be a first member, a member which is not itself caused by any preceding member—an uncaused or "first" cause.

It has frequently been pointed out that even if this argument were sound it would not establish the existence of *God*. It would not show that the first cause is all-powerful or all-good or that it is in any sense personal. Somebody believing in the eternity of atoms, or of matter generally, could quite consistently accept the conclusion. Defenders of the causal argument usually concede this and insist that the argument is not in itself meant to prove the existence of God. Supplementary arguments are required to show that the first cause must have the attributes assigned to the deity. They claim, however, that the argument, if valid, would at least be an important step towards a complete proof of the existence of God.

Does the argument succeed in proving so much as a first cause? This will depend mainly on the soundness of the premise that an infinite series of causes is impossible. Aquinas supports this premise by maintaining that the opposite belief involves a plain absurdity. To suppose that there is an infinite series of causes logically implies that nothing exists now; but we know that plenty of things do exist now; and hence any theory which implies that nothing exists now must be wrong. Let us take some causal series and refer to its members by the letters of the alphabet:

$$A \longrightarrow B \ldots W \longrightarrow X \longrightarrow Y \longrightarrow Z$$

Z stands here for something presently existing, e.g. Margaret Truman. Y represents the cause or part of the cause of Z, say Harry Truman. X designates the cause or part of the cause of Y, say Harry Truman's father, etc. Now, Aquinas reasons, whenever we take away the cause, we also take away the effect: if Harry Truman had never lived, Margaret Truman would never have been born. If Harry Truman's father had never lived, Harry Truman and Margaret Truman would never have been born. If A had never existed, none of the subsequent members of the series would have come into existence. But it is precisely A that the believer in the infinite series is "taking away." For in maintaining that the series is infinite he is denying that it has a first member; he is denying that there is such a thing as a first cause; he is in other words denying the existence of A. Since without A, Z could not have existed, his position implies that Z does not exist now; and that is plainly false.

This argument fails to do justice to the supporter of the infinite series of causes. Aquinas has failed to distinguish between the two statements:

(1) A did not exist, and
(2) A is not uncaused.

To say that the series is infinite implies (2), but it does not imply (1). The following parallel may be helpful here: Suppose Captain Spaulding had said, "I am the greatest explorer who ever lived," and somebody replied, "No, you are not." This answer would be denying that the Captain possessed the exalted attribute he had claimed for himself, but it would not be denying his existence. It would not be "taking him away." Similarly, the believer in the infinite series is not "taking A away." He is taking away the privileged status of A; he is taking away its "first causiness." He does not deny the *existence* of A or of any particular member of the series. He denies that A or anything else *is the first member* of the series. Since he is not taking A away, he is not taking B away, and thus he is also not taking X, Y, or Z away. His view, then, does not commit him to the absurdity that nothing exists now, or more specifically, that Margaret Truman does not exist now. It may be noted in this connection that a believer in the infinite series is not necessarily denying the existence of supernatural beings. He is merely committed to denying that such a being, if it exists, is uncaused. He is committed to holding that whatever other impressive attributes a supernatural being might possess, the attribute of being a first cause is not among them.

The causal argument is open to several other objections. Thus, even if otherwise valid, the argument would not prove a *single* first cause. For there does not seem to be any good ground for supposing that the various causal series in the universe ultimately merge. Hence even if it is granted that no series of causes can be infinite the possibility of a plurality of first members has not been ruled out. Nor does the argument establish the *present* existence of the first cause. It does not prove this, since experience clearly shows that an effect may exist long after its cause has been destroyed.

III

Many defenders of the causal argument would contend that at least some of these criticisms rest on a misunderstanding. They would probably go further and contend that the argument was not quite fairly stated in the first place—or at any rate that if it was fair to some of its adherents it was not fair to others. They would in this connection distinguish between two types of causes—what they call "causes *in fieri*" and what they call "causes *in esse*." A cause *in fieri* is a factor which brought or helped to bring an effect into existence. A cause *in esse* is a factor which "sustains" or helps to sustain the effect "in being." The parents of a human being would be an example of a cause *in fieri*. If somebody puts a book in my hand and I keep holding it up, his putting it there would be the cause *in fieri*, and my holding it would be the cause *in esse* of the book's position. To quote Father [G. H.] Joyce:

> If a smith forges a horse-shoe, he is only a cause *in fieri* of the shape given to the iron. That shape persists after his action has ceased. So, too, a builder is a cause *in fieri* of the house which he builds. In both these cases the substances employed act as causes *in esse* as regards the continued existence of the effect produced. Iron, in virtue of its natural rigidity, retains in being the shape which it has once received; and, similarly, the materials employed in building retain in being the order and arrangement which constitute them into a house.[9]

Using this distinction, a defender of the argument now reasons in the following way. To say that there is an infinite series of causes *in fieri* does not lead to any absurd conclusions. But Aquinas is concerned only with causes *in esse* and an infinite series of *such* causes is impossible. In the words of the contemporary American Thomist, R. P. Phillips:

> Each member of the series of causes possesses being solely by virtue of the actual present operation of a superior cause. . . . Life is dependent, *inter alia*, on a certain atmospheric pressure, this again on the continual operation of physical forces, whose being and operation depends on the position of the earth in the solar system, which itself must endure relatively unchanged, a state of being which can only be continuously produced by a definite—if unknown—constitution of the material universe. This constitution, however, cannot be its own cause. That a thing should cause itself is impossible: for in order that it may cause it is necessary for it to exist, which it cannot do,

[9] *The Principles of Natural Theology*, p. 58.

on the hypothesis, until it has been caused. So it must *be* in order to cause itself. Thus, not being uncaused nor yet its own cause, it must be caused by another, which produces and preserves it. It is plain, then, that as no member of this series possesses being except in virtue of the actual present operation of a superior cause, if there be no first cause actually operating none of the dependent causes could operate either. We are thus irresistibly led to posit a first efficient cause which, while itself uncaused, shall impart causality to a whole series. . . .

The series of causes which we are considering is not one which stretches back into the past; so that we are not demanding a beginning of the world at some definite moment reckoning back from the present, but an actual cause now operating, to account for the present being of things.[10]

Professor Phillips offers the following parallel to bring out his point:

In a goods train each truck is moved and moves by the action of the one immediately in front of it. If then we suppose the train to be infinite, i.e. that there is no end to it, and so no engine which starts the motion, it is plain that no truck will move. To lengthen it out to infinity will not give it what no member of it possesses of itself, viz. the power of drawing the truck behind it. If then we see any truck in motion we know there must be an end to the series of trucks which gives causality to the whole.[11]

Father Joyce introduces an illustration from Aquinas to explain how the present existence of things may be compatible with an infinite series of causes *in fieri* but not with an infinite series of causes *in esse*.

[10] *Modern Thomistic Philosophy*, Vol. II, pp. 284–85.
[11] *Op. cit.*, p. 278.

When a carpenter is at work, the series of efficient causes on which his work depends is necessarily limited. The final effect, e.g. the fastening of a nail is caused by a hammer: the hammer is moved by the arm: and the motion of his arm is determined by the motor-impulses communicated from the nerve centres of the brain. Unless the subordinate causes were limited in number, and were connected with a starting-point of motion, the hammer must remain inert; and the nail will never be driven in. If the series be supposed infinite, no work will ever take place. But if there is question of causes on which the work is not essentially dependent, we cannot draw the same conclusion. We may suppose the carpenter to have broken an infinite number of hammers, and as often to have replaced the broken tool by a fresh one. There is nothing in such a supposition which excludes the driving home of the nail.[12]

The supporter of the infinite series of causes, Joyce also remarks, is

. . . asking us to believe that although each link in a suspended chain is prevented from falling simply because it is attached to the one above it, yet if only the chain be long enough, it will, taken as a whole, need no support, but will hang loose in the air suspended from nothing.[13]

This formulation of the causal argument unquestionably circumvents one of the objections mentioned previously. If Y is the cause *in esse* of an effect, Z, then it must exist as long as Z exists. If the argument were valid in this form it would therefore prove the present and not merely the past existence of a first cause. In this form the argument is, however, less convincing in another respect. To maintain that all "natural" or

[12] *Op. cit.,* pp. 67–68.
[13] *Op. cit.,* p. 82.

"phenomenal" objects—things like tables and mountains and human beings—require a cause *in fieri* is not implausible, though even here Mill and others have argued that strictly speaking only *changes* require a causal explanation. It is far from plausible, on the other hand, to claim that all natural objects require a cause *in esse*. It may be granted that the air around us is a cause *in esse* of human life and further that certain gravitational forces are among the causes *in esse* of the air being where it is. But when we come to gravitational forces or, at any rate, to material particles like atoms or electrons it is difficult to see what cause *in esse* they require. To those not already convinced of the need for a supernatural First Cause some of the remarks by Professor Phillips in this connection appear merely dogmatic and question-begging. Most people would grant that such particles as atoms did not cause themselves, since, as Professor Phillips observes, they would in that event have had to exist before they began existing. It is not at all evident, however, that these particles cannot be uncaused. Professor Phillips and all other supporters of the causal argument immediately proceed to claim that there is something else which needs no cause *in esse*. They themselves admit thus, that there is nothing self-evident about the proposition that everything must have a cause *in esse*. Their entire procedure here lends substance to Schopenhauer's gibe that supporters of the cosmological argument treat the law of universal causation like "a hired cab which we dismiss when we have reached our destination."[14]

---

[14] *The Fourfold Root of the Principle of Sufficient Reason*, pp. 42–43. My attention to this passage was drawn by Professor C. J. Ducasse. See his excellent discussion of the arguments for the existence of God in *A Philosophical Scrutiny of Religion*, Chapter 15.

But waiving this and all similar objections, the re-statement of the argument in terms of causes *in esse* in no way avoids the main difficulty which was previously mentioned. A believer in the infinite series would insist that his position was just as much misrepresented now as before. He is no more removing the member of the series which is supposed to be the first cause *in esse* than he was removing the member which had been declared to be the first cause *in fieri*. He is again merely denying a privileged status to it. He is not denying the reality of the cause *in esse* labelled "A." He is not even necessarily denying that it possesses supernatural attributes. He is again merely taking away its "first causiness."

The advocates of the causal argument in either form seem to confuse an infinite series with one which is long but finite. If a book, Z, is to remain in its position, say 100 miles up in the air, there must be another object, say another book, Y, underneath it to serve as its support. If Y is to remain where it is, it will need another support, X, beneath it. Suppose that this series of supports, one below the other, continues for a long time, but eventually, say after 100,000 members, comes to a first book which is not resting on any other book or indeed on any other support. In that event the whole collection would come crashing down. What we seem to need is a first member of the series, a first support (such as the earth) which does not need another member as *its* support, which in other words is "self-supporting."

This is evidently the sort of picture that supporters of the First Cause argument have before their minds when they rule out the possibility of an infinite series. But such a picture is not a fair representation of the theory of the infinite series. A *finite* series of books would indeed come crashing down, since the first or lowest member would not have a predecessor on which it could be supported. If the series, however, were infinite this would not be the case. In that event every member *would* have a predecessor to support itself on and there would be no crash. That is to say: a crash can be avoided either by a finite series with a first self-supporting member or by an infinite series. Similarly, the present existence of motion is equally compatible with the theory of a first unmoved mover and with the theory of an infinite series of moving objects; and the present existence of causal activity is compatible with the theory of a first cause *in esse* as much as with the theory of an infinite series of such causes.

The illustrations given by Joyce and Phillips are hardly to the point. It is true that a carpenter would not, *in a finite time-span*, succeed in driving in a nail if he had to carry out an infinite number of movements. For that matter, he would not accomplish this goal in a finite time if he broke an infinite number of hammers. However, to make the illustrations relevant we must suppose that he has infinite time at his disposal. In that case he would succeed in driving in the nail even if he required an infinite number of movements for this purpose. As for the goods train, it may be granted that the trucks do not move unless the train has an engine. But this illustration is totally irrelevant as it stands. A relevant illustration would be that of engines, each moved by the one in front of it. Such a train would move if it were infinite. For every member of this series there would be one in front capable of drawing it along. The advocate of the infinite series of causes does not, as the original illustration suggests, believe in a series whose members are not really causally connected with one another. In the series he believes in every member is genuinely the cause of the one that follows it.

IV

No staunch defender of the cosmological argument would give up at this stage. Even if there were an infinite series of causes *in fieri* or *in esse*, he would contend, this still would not do away with the need for an ultimate, a first cause. As Father Copleston put it in his debate with Bertrand Russell:

> Every object has a phenomenal cause, if you insist on the infinity of the series. But the series of phenomenal causes is an insufficient explanation of the series. Therefore, the series has not a phenomenal cause, but a transcendent cause. . . .[15]
>
> An infinite series of contingent beings will be, to my way of thinking, as unable to cause itself as one contingent being.[16]

The demand to find the cause of the series as a whole rests on the erroneous assumption that the series is something over and above the members of which it is composed. It is tempting to suppose this, at least by implication, because the word "series" is a noun like "dog" or "man." Like the expression "this dog" or "this man" the phrase "this series" is easily taken to designate an individual object. But reflection shows this to be an error. If we have explained the individual members there is nothing additional left to be explained. Supposing I see a group of five Eskimos standing on the corner of Sixth Avenue and 50th Street and

---

[15] *Why I Am Not a Christian*, pp. 152–53.
[16] *Ibid.*, p. 151.

I wish to explain why the group came to New York. Investigation reveals the following stories:

> Eskimo No. 1 did not enjoy the extreme cold in the polar region and decided to move to a warmer climate.
>
> No. 2 is the husband of Eskimo No. 1. He loves her dearly and did not wish to live without her.
>
> No. 3 is the son of Eskimos 1 and 2. He is too small and too weak to oppose his parents.
>
> No. 4 saw an advertisement in the *New York Times* for an Eskimo to appear on television.
>
> No. 5 is a private detective engaged by the Pinkerton Agency to keep an eye on Eskimo No. 4.

Let us assume that we have now explained in the case of each of the five Eskimos why he or she is in New York. Somebody then asks: "All right, but what about the group as a whole; why is *it* in New York?" This would plainly be an absurd question. There is no group over and above the five members, and if we have explained why each of the five members is in New York we have *ipso facto* explained why the group is there. It is just as absurd to ask for the cause of the series as a whole as distinct from asking for the causes of individual members.

V

It is most unlikely that a determined defender of the cosmological line of reasoning would surrender even here. He would probably admit that the series is not a thing over and above its members and that it does not make sense to ask for the cause of the series if the cause of each member has already been found. He would insist, however, that when he asked for the explanation of the entire series, he was not asking for its *cause*. He was really saying that a series, finite or infinite, is not "intelligible" or "explained" if it consists of nothing but "contingent" members. To quote Father Copleston once more:

> What we call the world is intrinsically unintelligible apart from the existence of God. The infinity of the series of events, if such an infinity could be proved, would not be in the slightest degree relevant to the situation. If you add up chocolates, you get chocolates after all, and not a sheep. If you add up chocolates to infinity, you presumably get an infinite number of chocolates. So, if you add up contingent beings to infinity, you still get contingent beings, not a necessary being.[17]

This last quotation is really a summary of the "contingency argument," the other main form of the cosmological proof and the third of the five ways of Aquinas. It may be stated more fully in these words: All around us we perceive contingent beings. This includes all physical objects and also all human minds. In calling them "contingent" we mean that they might not have existed. We mean that the universe can be *conceived* without this or that physical object, without this or that human being, however certain their actual existence may be. These contingent beings we can trace back to other contingent beings—e.g. a human being to his parents. However, since these other beings are also contingent, they do not provide a real or full explanation. The contingent beings we originally wanted explained have not yet become intelligible, since the beings to which they have been traced back are no more necessary than they were. It is just as true of our parents, for example, as it is of ourselves, that they

[17] *Op. cit.*, p. 151.

might not have existed. We can then properly explain the contingent beings around us only by tracing them back ultimately to some necessary being, to something which exists necessarily, which has "the reason for its existence within itself." The existence of contingent beings, in other words, implies the existence of a necessary being.

This form of the cosmological argument is even more beset with difficulties than the causal variety. In the first place, there is the objection, stated with great force by Kant, that it really commits the same error as the ontological argument in tacitly regarding existence as an attribute or characteristic. To say that there is a necessary being is to say that it would be a self-contradiction to deny its existence. This would mean that at least one existential statement is a necessary truth; and this in turn presupposes that in at least one case existence is contained in a concept. But only a characteristic can be contained in a concept and it has seemed plain to most philosophers since Kant that existence is not a characteristic, that it can hence never be contained in a concept, and that hence no existential statement can ever be a necessary truth. To talk about anything "existing necessarily" is in their view about as sensible as to talk about round squares, and they have concluded that the contingency-argument is quite absurd.

It would lead too far to discuss here the reasons for denying that existence is a characteristic. I will assume that this difficulty can somehow be surmounted and that the expression "necessary being," as it is intended by the champions of the contingency-argument, might conceivably apply to something. There remain other objections which are of great weight. I shall try to state these by first quoting again from the debate between Bertrand Russell and Father Copleston:

RUSSELL: . . . It all turns on this question of sufficient reason, and I must say you haven't defined "sufficient reason" in a way that I can understand—what do you mean by sufficient reason? You don't mean cause?

COPLESTON: Not necessarily. Cause is a kind of sufficient reason. Only contingent being can have a cause. God is his own sufficient reason; and he is not cause of himself. By sufficient reason in the full sense I mean an explanation adequate for the existence of some particular being.

RUSSELL: But when is an explanation adequate? Suppose I am about to make a flame with a match. You may say that the adequate explanation of that is that I rub it on the box.

COPLESTON: Well for practical purposes—but theoretically, that is only a partial explanation. An adequate explanation must ultimately be a total explanation, to which nothing further can be added.

RUSSELL: Then I can only say that you're looking for something which can't be got, and which one ought not to expect to get.

COPLESTON: To say that one has not found it is one thing; to say that one should not look for it seems to me rather dogmatic.

RUSSELL: Well, I don't know. I mean, the explanation of one thing is another thing which makes the other thing dependent on yet another, and you have to grasp this sorry scheme of things entire to do what you want, and that we can't do.[18]

Russell's main point here may be expanded in the following way. The contingency-argument rests on a misconception of what an explanation is and does, and similarly on what it is that makes phenomena "intel-

[18] *Op. cit.*, p. 150.

ligible." Or else it involves an obscure and arbitrary redefinition of "explanation," "intelligible," and related terms. Normally, we are satisfied that we have explained a phenomenon if we have found its cause or if we have exhibited some other uniform or near-uniform connection between it and something else. Confining ourselves to the former case, which is probably the most common, we might say that a phenomenon, Z, has been explained if it has been traced back to a group of factors, a, b, c, d, etc., which are its cause. These factors are the full and real explanation of Z, quite regardless of whether they are pleasing or displeasing, admirable or contemptible, necessary or contingent. The explanation would not be adequate only if the factors listed are not really the cause of Z. If they are the cause of Z, the explanation would be adequate, even though each of the factors is merely a "contingent" being.

Let us suppose that we have been asked to explain why General Eisenhower won the elections of 1952. "He was an extremely popular general," we might answer, "while Stevenson was relatively little known; moreover there was a great deal of resentment over the scandals in the Truman Administration." If somebody complained that this was only a partial explanation we might mention additional antecedents, such as the widespread belief that the Democrats had allowed communist agents to infiltrate the State Department, that Eisenhower was a man with a winning smile, and that unlike Stevenson he had shown the good sense to say one thing on race relations in the North and quite another in the South. Theoretically, we might go further and list the motives of all American voters during the weeks or months preceding the elections. If we could do this we would have explained Eisenhower's victory. We would have made it intelligible. We would "understand" why he won and why Stevenson lost. Perhaps there is a sense in which we might make Eisenhower's victory even more intelligible if we went further back and discussed such matters as the origin of American views on Communism or of racial attitudes in the North and South. However, to explain the outcome of the election in any ordinary sense, loose or strict, it would not be necessary to go back to prehistoric days or to the amœba or to a first cause, if such a first cause exists. Nor would our explanation be considered in any way defective because each of the factors mentioned was a "contingent" and not a necessary being. The only thing that matters is whether the factors were really the cause of Eisenhower's election. If they were, then it has been explained although they are contingent beings. If they were not the cause of Eisenhower's victory, we would have failed to explain it even if each of the factors were a necessary being.

If it is granted that, in order to explain a phenomenon or to make it intelligible, we need not bring in a necessary being, then the contingency-argument breaks down. For a series, as was already pointed out, is not something over and above its members; and every contingent member of it could in that case be explained by reference to other contingent beings. But I should wish to go further than this and it is evident from Russell's remarks that he would do so also. Even if it were granted, both that the phrase "necessary being" is meaningful and that all explanations are defective unless the phenomena to be explained are traced back to a necessary being, the conclusion would still not have been established. The conclusion follows from this premise together with the additional premise that *there are* explanations of phenomena in the special sense just mentioned. It is this further premise which Russell (and many other philosophers) would question. They do not merely question, as Copleston implies, whether human beings can ever obtain explanations in this sense, but whether they *exist*. To assume without further ado that phenomena have explanations or an explanation in this sense is to beg the very point at issue. The use of the same word "explanation" in two crucially different ways lends the additional premise a plausibility it does not really possess. It may indeed be highly plausible to assert that phenomena have explanations, whether we have found them or not, in the ordinary sense in which this usually means that they have causes. It is then tempting to suppose, because of the use of the same word, that they also have explanations in a sense in which this implies dependence on a necessary being. But this is a gross *non sequitur*.

VI

It is necessary to add a few words about the proper way of formulating the position of those who reject the main premise of the cosmological argument, in either of the forms we have considered. It is sometimes maintained in this connection that in order to reach a "self-existing" entity it is not necessary to go beyond the universe: the universe itself (or "Nature") is "self-existing." And this in turn is sometimes expanded into the statement that while all individual things "within" the universe are caused, the universe itself is uncaused. Statements of this kind are found in Büchner, Bradlaugh, Haeckel, and other free-thinkers of the nineteenth and early twentieth century. Sometimes the assertion that the universe is "self-existing" is elaborated to mean that *it* is the "necessary being." Some eighteenth-century unbelievers, apparently accepting the view that there is a necessary being, asked why Nature or the material universe could not fill the bill as well or better than God.

> "Why," asks one of the characters in Hume's *Dialogues*, "may not the material universe be the necessarily existent Being? . . . We dare not affirm that we know all the qualities of matter; and for aught we can determine, it may contain some qualities, which, were they known, would make its non-existence appear as great a contradiction as that twice two is five."[19]

Similar remarks can be found in Holbach and several of the Encyclopedists.

The former of these formulations immediately invites the question why the universe, alone of all "things," is exempted from the universal sway of causation. "The strong point of the cosmological argument," writes Dr. Ewing, "is that after all it does remain incredible that the physical universe should just have happened. . . . It calls out for some further explanation of some kind."[20] The latter formulation is exposed to the criticism that there is nothing any more "necessary" about the existence of the universe or Nature as a whole than about any particular thing within the universe.

I hope some of the earlier discussions in this article have made it clear that in rejecting the cosmological

[19] *Op. cit.*, Part IX.
[20] *Op. cit.*, p. 225.

argument one is not committed to either of these propositions. If I reject the view that there is a supernatural first cause, I am not thereby committed to the proposition that there is a *natural* first cause, and even less to the proposition that a mysterious "thing" called "the universe" qualifies for this title. I may hold that there is no "universe" over and above individual things of various sorts; and, accepting the causal principle, I may proceed to assert that all these things are caused by other things, and these other things by yet other things, and so on, *ad infinitum*. In this way no arbitrary exception is made to the principle of causation. Similarly, if I reject the assertion that God is a "necessary being," I am not committed to the view that the universe is such an entity. I may hold that it does not make sense to speak of anything as a "necessary being" and that even if there were such a thing as the universe it could not be properly considered a necessary being.

However, in saying that nothing is uncaused or that there is no necessary being, one is not committed to the view that everything, or for that matter anything, is merely a "brute fact." Dr. Ewing laments that "the usual modern philosophical views opposed to theism do not try to give any rational explanation of the world at all, but just take it as a brute fact not to be explained." They thus fail to "rationalize" the universe. Theism, he concedes, cannot completely rationalize things either since it does not show "how God can be his own cause or how it is that he does not need a cause."[21] Now, if one means by "brute fact" something for which there *exists* no explanation (as distinct from something for which no explanation is in our possession), then the theists have at least one brute fact

[21] *Op. cit.*, p. 225.

on their hands, namely God. Those who adopt Büchner's formulation also have one brute fact on their hands, namely "the universe." Only the position I have been supporting dispenses with brute facts altogether. I don't know if this is any special virtue, but the defenders of the cosmological argument seem to think so.

2. Alvin Plantinga (1932–)

[Alvin Plantinga is Associate Professor of Philosophy
at Wayne State University, Detroit, Michigan. He has
written a number of papers in the area of linguistic
analysis and religion. Here he is concerned with the
meaning attached to the notion of God as *Necessary
Being,* and he maintains that the proposition "God
exists" is neither analytic nor logically necessary, but
rather supports a series of propositions whose meanings are in accord with the conceptual schema of
Hebraic-Christian theism. He further attempts to show
why assertions concerning God's existence or non-
existence have no relevance to questions normally ascribed to causality, and why, therefore, the notion of
Necessary Being is applicable to the conception of
God.]

Necessary Being*

It is often said that the important philosophical
questions about religious belief are not questions of
proof but questions of meaning. The skeptic used to
insist that "it is wrong always, everywhere, and for
anyone, to believe anything upon insufficient evi-

* From *Faith and Philosophy,* edited by Alvin Plantinga
(Grand Rapids, 1964). Reprinted by permission of Wm. B.
Eerdmans Publishing Co.

dence"[1] and that the evidence for religious or theological teachings is insufficient indeed; he now claims that the teachings themselves are logically questionable or out of order or even senseless. A case in point is the assertion that God is the *necessary being*. Theologians and religious persons do say in fact that God is the necessary being. In this respect, they say, God is to be contrasted with all other beings whatever; these others are merely *contingent*. Some have argued that from the very concept of God it follows that He is a necessary being; and a necessary being, they point out, necessarily exists.[2] On the other hand, it has been argued that God must indeed be a necessary being . . . but since the concept of necessary being is self-contradictory, God necessarily does not exist.[3] And many philosophers have claimed that the locution "necessary being" is a piece of straight nonsense; hence if there is a God, He cannot possibly be a necessary being. The claim that God is the necessary being, then, is troublesome. My purpose in this paper is to discover whether that claim can be construed in a way which is both logically proper and religiously adequate.

What requirements must a "religiously adequate" account of necessary being meet? First, by "religiously adequate" I mean "adequate to the demands of the Christian religion." The doctrine that God is the necessary being perhaps occurs in other religions as well,

[1] W. K. Clifford, "The Ethics of Belief," *Lectures and Essays* (London, 1901).

[2] Anselm, in one formulation of the ontological argument. Cf. N. Malcolm, "Anselm's Ontological Arguments," *Philosophical Review* (January 1960).

[3] J. N. Findlay, "Can God's Existence Be Disproved?" *Mind* (1949). Reprinted in *New Essays in Philosophical Theology*, edited by Antony Flew and Alasdair MacIntyre (London, 1955).

particularly in Judaism and Islam. But whether this is so is not my concern here. So to see what requirements a religiously adequate account of God's necessity must meet, we must see what it is about Christianity that leads the believer to hold this doctrine. The answer is at least twofold. First, there is the pressure in theistic religions to ascribe *unlimited superiority* to God. The object of worship (as opposed to surpassing admiration or limitless respect), God is not merely very great; He is the greatest of all beings. Nor is He merely the greatest of all beings as a matter of fact; God is the greatest possible being; He is "that than which none greater can be conceived." Now mere creatures have, so to speak, a tenuous and uneasy hold upon their existence. They are made by God and can be unmade by Him. They exist only by courtesy and their continued existence depends upon the continued favor of their creator. And God's superiority to His creatures is manifested, not merely in the fact that this dependence is not reciprocal, but in the fact that He alone has always existed, will always exist, cannot cease to exist. "From everlasting to everlasting, thou art."[4]

A second feature of Christian theism leads to the same conclusion. For the believer, God is the being in whom *absolute trust* may be placed; He is an invincible and utterly reliable ally. Earthly fathers, in spite of good intentions, may fail in various ways; but the Heavenly Father cannot be defeated by any eventuality whatever. Earthly parents are sometimes thwarted in their efforts, and as the child discovers to his dismay, parents are subject to death. But God differs from any earthly parent in just this respect; noth-

---

[4] See Findlay's article mentioned above. Findlay puts this very well.

ing can thwart His purposes, and the threat of non-existence does not confront Him. Hence, the believer claims, God exists in some necessary manner; He *cannot* cease to exist. These two features of Christian theism (and perhaps others as well) lead the believer to assert that God is the necessary being. A religiously adequate account of God's necessity, therefore, must allow the believer to say, in some non-Pickwickian sense of "cannot," that God cannot cease existing.

An example of an account of God's necessity that does not seem to meet this requirement is to be found in J. J. C. Smart's "The Existence of God."[5] After asserting that the existence of God cannot be *logically* necessary, Smart makes the following suggestion:

> I think I can see roughly what sort of necessity theological necessity might be. Let me give an analogy from physics. It is not a logical necessity that the velocity of light in a vacuum should be constant. It would, however, upset physical theory considerably if we denied it. Similarly it is not a logical necessity that God exists. But it would clearly upset the structure of our religious attitudes in the most violent way if we denied it or even entertained the possibility of its falsehood.[6]

It is indeed true that the believer's attitude of worship would be upset in the most violent way if he denied or were doubtful of the existence of God. Engaging in Christian worship without believing in God is like admitting that Pegasus is a mere myth while eagerly scanning the heavens for a glimpse of him. The belief that God exists is a presupposition of the Christian's entire religious enterprise. But contrary to the apparent intent of Smart's suggestion, when the be-

[5] *Church Quarterly Review* (1955). Reprinted in Flew and MacIntyre, *op. cit.*

[6] In Flew and MacIntyre, *op. cit.*, p. 40.

liever says that God is the necessary being he is not, surely, uttering the mere truism that his religious attitudes would be upset if he ceased to believe in God. For it is quite in accord with theism to admit the possibility of persons who believe that God is the necessary being and yet have no religious attitudes at all. "The devils also believe, and they tremble."[7] And one of the things the devils might well believe is that God is the necessary being; but, of course, there is no question of *their* religious attitudes being upset. More importantly, on Smart's account the assertion of God's necessity becomes an assertion about believers and their religious attitudes rather than an assertion about God. His account does not allow the believer to assert straightforwardly that God cannot cease to exist; and it thereby fails to do justice to the concept of necessary existence.

I

If Smart's explanation won't do, how *are* we to construe the assertion that God is the necessary being?

It has been argued that to speak of necessary *beings* (or for that matter of contingent beings) is to talk egregious nonsense. Locutions such as "necessary" and "contingent," so the claim goes, apply properly to statements or propositions only; to speak of a necessary being is like speaking of an unpunctual triangle. Argument for this view is distressingly scarce, however, and it is accordingly difficult to evaluate. But even if the proscription upon the phrase "necessary being" is correct, the theist will be happy to oblige, presumably, by holding instead that the statement

[7] James 2:19.

"God exists" is necessary. We may begin by examining that claim.

A fashionable view has it that a statement or proposition is necessary if and only if it is analytic. Whether that view is correct is a matter of controversy; but at any rate it is clear that all analytic propositions are necessary. We shall first inquire, therefore, whether the proposition "God exists" is analytic. And for present purposes a proposition is analytic if and only if its denial is self-contradictory. Now our proposition does not, at first glance anyway, seem to be analytic, for the proposition "God does not exist" does not seem to be contradictory. Indeed, many philosophers and even some theologians have cheerfully accepted the proposition that God does not exist. And this apparently leads J. N. Findlay to believe that "God exists" is not analytic, on the grounds, presumably, that if it were, no one who seriously considered it would deny it.[8] But, of course, often there *is* sensible disagreement as to whether a given proposition is analytic. Leaving aside such cases as complicated mathematical and logical propositions, we might note the controversy as to whether one can consistently assert the existence of a logically private language. Hence the fact that "God exists" does not prima facie appear analytic by no means settles the question. What is needed is some sort of argument to *show* that it is not analytic.

And such argument, I think, can be provided. Let us begin by recognizing a class of statements which assert or entail the existence of a thing or things of some specified kind, e.g., "There are female cab-drivers," or "Some children are very noisy." We may

[8] *Op. cit.* See especially pp. 48 and 54. See also G. B. Hughes' comments on Findlay's paper, in Flew and MacIntyre, *op. cit.*, pp. 61, 62.

refer to statements of this sort as "existential statements" and to their contradictories as "contra-existential statements." In making an existential statement, I assert that there is at least one thing which satisfies a certain description. Now it often happens that the description in question is complex in the sense that it comprises several logically independent properties or characteristics.[9] And if it is complex (as is, e.g., the description implied by "centaur"), then my assertion that at least one thing satisfies that description entails that at least one thing has all of the properties included in the description. If I say, "There are some centaurs," I am saying that there is at least one thing which has each of the properties included in the connotation of "centaur." My statement, therefore, entails that certain statements of the form "A has F" are true where what replaces "A" refers to some specific individual which in fact has all of the properties comprising the connotation of "centaur" and where "F" may be replaced by the names of those properties. Some of these statements would be the following: "A has a human head," "A has a human chest," "A has an equine lower body," etc. Some existential statements, therefore, are complex in the sense that they entail several logically independent propositions of the above form.

It is for this reason, of course, that existential statements may be self-contradictory. For our purposes, a self-contradictory statement may be characterized as one which entails two statements such that one of the entailed statements is the denial of the other. "Jones is a married bachelor," for example, entails that Jones

---

[9] Properties A and B are logically independent if the statement that X has A neither entails nor is entailed by the statement that X has B.

is married and also that Jones is not married; similarly such existential statements as "There are round squares" or "There are octogenarians under fifty years of age" are contradictory.

Contra-existential statements, on the other hand, are not in this sense complex. Suppose the connotation of "centaur" is comprised by properties A, B, C, D. In asserting that there are no centaurs I am not, of course, asserting that there are no individuals with the property A. I am not, for example, asserting that nothing has the head of a man, or an equine lower body. What I am asserting is only that no individual satisfies the description in question by having *all* the properties comprising the connotation of "centaur"; I am saying that there is nothing which is ABCD. But that statement is not complex. For it may be regarded as asserting, of each individual, that either it is non-A or non-B or non-C or non-D (where "X is non-A" is to mean the same as "X is not A"). And the truth of any instantiation of such a statement requires only that *one* of its disjuncts be true. But if so, the statement in question does not and cannot entail *two* statements one of which is the denial of the other; hence it cannot be contradictory. And of course the point may be put more generally; to deny that there are any X's is to assert that no individual has all of the properties comprising the connotation of "X." But such an assertion is not complex in the above sense and cannot, therefore, be contradictory. And if no contra-existential statement is contradictory, no existential statement is analytic; accordingly, "God exists" is not analytic.

An objection might be directed against the *specific* thesis that the statement "God exists" is not analytic: if "is a man" is one of the properties included in the connotation of "bachelor," to deny that bachelors are men would be contradictory. So, if "is existent" is one of the properties included in the connotation of the term "God," it would be contradictory to deny that God exists. And, the argument might proceed, existence *is* one of the properties included in the concept of God. This line has been familiar since Anselm. And the answer, traditional since Kant, is that existence is not a property; it cannot, therefore, be one of the properties included in the connotation of "God." Kant's answer, someone might say, takes too short a way with Anselm's argument. For when I say "This chair exists," I am surely saying something that might not have been true; since what I say *is* true, I am saying something about *something;* and if not about this chair, then about what? But if I can say something about a chair by saying that it exists, there is good reason to hold that existence *is* a property or predicate.[10]

This argument is wrong on more than one count. But even if existence *is* a property, it is a property of a very special sort, and the features that distinguish it from other properties are just what make it impossible that existential statements be analytic. That this is the case may be suggested in the following way: Any synthetic non-existential statement of subject predicate form may be turned into an analytic statement by the simple expedient of redefining the subject term in such a way that the property mentioned in the predicate is annexed to the connotation of the subject term. For example, the statement, "All crows are black" (taken non-existentially), can be made analytic simply

[10] Cf. G. E. Moore, "Is Existence a Predicate?" *Proceedings of the Aristotelian Society,* Supplementary Volume XV (1936). Reprinted in *Logic and Language,* 2d series edited by A. Flew (Oxford, 1953), pp. 92–93.

by annexing "black" to the normal connotation of "crow"; the proposition then says what "All black crows are black" says when the terms involved have their usual meanings. In like fashion we can convert "All potatoes are edible" into an analytic statement by adding "edible" to the normal connotation of potato. (A similar procedure can be specified for statements that do not yield to subject predicate analysis.) But existential statements cannot be made analytic by redefinition in this way. Consider, for example, the statement, "There are centaurs." Can this statement be rendered analytic by redefinition? Let's try. Presumably the thing to do is to annex the property of existence, ascribed to centaurs by the statement in question, to the connotation of "centaur." "Centaur" in our redefined sense means what "existent centaur" ordinarily means. "There are centaurs" then comes to "There are existent centaurs." Is that proposition analytic? It does not seem so. For the difference between a centaur and an existent centaur is far from clear. It might be argued that to say "Centaurs exist" and to say "Existent centaurs exist" is to say the same thing. And if so, of course there would be no contradiction in denying that there are existent centaurs. But even if there is a difference between centaurs and existent centaurs, even if the adjective "existent" marks off some special class of centaurs (e.g., existent centaurs as opposed to merely imaginary ones), we can still deny that there are existent centaurs without contradiction, for we can consistently deny that there are any centaurs at all. And if there are no centaurs at all, of course there are no existent ones. So the fact that existential propositions cannot be made analytic by redefinition indicates a crucial difference between existence, if it is a property at all, and other properties. It is in virtue of that difference, I suggest, that non-contradictory existential statements are all synthetic. It follows, then, that "God exists" is not analytic.

And if not analytic, it may be asked, in what sense necessary? Some philosophers hold that propositions expressing the incompatibility of certain colors, or the relational properties of certain tones, or certain spatial and temporal relations are necessary though not analytic. The proposition, "Nothing can be green and red all over at the same time," e.g., is sometimes said to be both synthetic and necessary. Is the assertion that God exists necessary in the way that such propositions are said to be? Surely not. For the distinguishing characteristic of synthetic necessary propositions, as explained by their defenders, is that their denials, while logically quite consistent, are nonetheless inconceivable. And the best evidence that "God exists" does not enjoy this characteristic is just that reasonable and intelligent people do in fact conceive its denial. This answer would be inappropriate to the suggestion that the proposition is analytic, for reasonable people do sometimes appear to hold beliefs revealed contradictory by subsequent investigation. But it is the best and only conclusive reply to the claim that though the statement in question is synthetic, its denial is nonetheless inconceivable. A secondary count against the claim is that all other propositions said to enjoy this status describe or report relationships between possible instances of two or more properties; none of them assert that any property *has* instances or that some description actually applies to anything. "Whatever is colored is extended" has been held to be both necessary and synthetic; that claim is not made for "There are colored objects." Hence, the claim that "God exists" is a synthetic necessary proposition is implausible.

The above discussion raises most acutely the question whether any meaning at all can be given to the assertion that God is the necessary being. In what follows, I shall try to explain the proposition that God is a necessary being in a way which is faithful to the conceptual scheme of theism but avoids the paradoxical conclusion that "God exists" is logically necessary.

II

We may begin by considering two somewhat peculiar questions. Suppose someone asked, "Why is it that all vacuums are empty?" The question is puzzling. It is indeed true and necessarily true that all vacuums are empty. But if the phrase, "Why is it that . . . ," is taken to have the same role here that it does in, say, "Why is it that there are craters on the moon?", then the question seems senseless, for there seems to be no sensible way of answering it. "They just are" won't do; that suggests that perhaps they might not have been. "I don't know" won't do as a reply either, for there is nothing here we don't know—there is no room for some unknown fact which would serve as an answer to the question. One might possibly use this sentence to ask why we use the word "vacuum" to designate spaces entirely devoid of matter; presumably many other sequences of letters would do as well. But that question is about speakers and language habits; it is not about vacuums at all. Again, the question might be a misleading way of asking for the conditions under which vacuums occur. And other reinterpretations could be suggested. But one who repudiated all such reinterpretations and insisted that he meant the question in a perfectly straightforward manner would betray misunderstanding of one or another of the concepts involved. For in the case of any analytic statement A, the words "Why is it that A?" do not express a genuine query; since there is no room for an answer (since nothing *could* serve as an answer), nothing is being asked.

Now let us consider a different sort of question. Suppose someone, struck by the fact that his desk might not have existed, asks, "Why is it that this desk exists?" Perhaps there are several sorts of reply we could give him. One answer might be that the desk exists because a certain carpenter made it. But suppose our questioner is still puzzled; the carpenter, he says, also might not have existed, so why did *he* exist? We could answer again by referring to some other beings or states of affairs which were causally sufficient for the existence of the carpenter; but of course, the same question will arise about these beings, and about the causes of these beings, and so indefinitely. No matter how far back we push this series of questions and answers, our questioner may remain dissatisfied. It may appear to us that he is looking for a *final* answer, one which allows no further questions of the same sort. He seems to be seeking an answer which shares with the analytic statement above the characteristic that it leaves no room for a question of the form, "Why is it that p?" And in order to put an end to the series of questions and answers which, as he claims, never will be able to satisfy him, he may ask, "But why does anything exist at all?"

This is the second unusual question I wish to consider. It *is* an unusual question both in the sense that it is asked by some people only, and then only in certain uncommon moods, and in the sense that it is not easy to see what kind of answer is required. Now the context in which the question arises might suggest that the questioner would be satisfied only with an answer referring to some being that never could fail to exist. And such a being would be a necessary being. But if the kind of necessity involved is *logical* necessity, then (if my previous argument is correct) there *could be* no such being and hence no answer to the question. J. J. C. Smart so interprets the question: ". . . now let us ask, 'Why should anything exist at all?' Logic seems to tell us that the only answer which is not absurd is to say, 'Why shouldn't it?' "[11] But, of course, that retort is a way of rejecting the question altogether; and Smart's argument that the question ought on logical grounds to be rejected rests upon the supposition that the question is "an absurd request for the nonsensical postulation of a logically necessary being."[12] But it need not be interpreted that way.

How then *is* it to be interpreted? Let us return to the context of the question. In asking "Why is there anything at all?" the questioner attempts to put an end to the indefinitely long series of questions and answers where the answer to each question mentions a being or state of affairs about which precisely the same question again may be asked. In seeking a *final* answer, he is seeking a statement which puts an end to the series of questions and answers. A necessary being, therefore, may be characterized as (a) a being such that some statement referring to it can serve as a final answer in this sort of question and answer series, an answer which puts an end to the series. But a final answer in the series would refer to a being of an unusual sort; such a being must be one about which

[11] *Op. cit.*, p. 46.
[12] *Ibid.*

the question "Why does it exist?" *does not arise* or cannot sensibly be asked. A necessary being, therefore, may be further characterized as (b) a being about which one cannot sensibly ask why it exists. But of course these two descriptions are not independent. For if a being satisfies description (a) it must also satisfy (b); the statement that a being satisfies (a) entails the statement that it satisfies (b). But similarly if the question "Why does X exist?" cannot sensibly be asked, then quite obviously some statement mentioning X can serve to put an end to the series of questions and answers under consideration. The entailment holds the other way as well. When the theist, therefore, asserts that God is the necessary being, we may construe his remark in the following way. He is pointing out that we cannot sensibly ask, "Why is it that God exists?" And he is holding that some assertion about God is the final answer in the series of questions and answers we have been considering.

Next, we should note that the question "Why does God exist?" never does, in fact, arise. Those who do not believe that God exists will not, of course, ask *why* He exists. But neither do believers ask that question. Outside of theism, so to speak, the question is nonsensical, and inside of theism, the question is never asked. But it is not that the religious person fails to ask why God exists through inadvertence or because of lack of interest. There may be many beings about which the question "Why do they exist?" is never *in fact* asked; and not all such beings are necessary in the sense in question. "Why does God exist?" is never in fact asked (either by religious or non-religious people) because it is a bogus question. If a believer were asked why God exists, he might take it as a request for his reasons for believing in God; but if it is agreed that God exists, then it is less than sensible to ask why He does. And the explanation is not hard to find. Essential to theism is an assertion to the effect that there is a connection between God and all other beings, a connection in virtue of which these others are causally dependent upon God. And this proposition is analytic; it is part of the Hebraic-Christian concept of God that He is "Maker of heaven and earth." But it is also a necessary truth that if God exists, He is Himself uncreated and in no way causally dependent upon anything else. God is a causally necessary condition of the existence of anything else, whereas His existence has no necessary conditions. Now the absence of a necessary condition of the existence of anything is a sufficient condition of the non-existence of that thing; and if a being has no causally necessary conditions, then its non-existence has no causally sufficient conditions. And hence if God does exist, His going out of existence could have no causally sufficient conditions and is therefore causally impossible. If God has no necessary conditions, then it is analytic that His going out of existence, if it occurred, would be an uncaused event; for it is analytic that there can be no causally sufficient conditions of its occurrence. Similarly, His beginning to exist is causally impossible, for since it is analytic that God is not dependent upon anything, He has no cause; and hence His coming into existence would be an event which could have no causally sufficient conditions. So if God does exist, He cannot cease to exist; nor could He have begun to exist.

Now it becomes clear that it is absurd to ask why God exists. To ask that question is to presuppose that God does exist; but it is a necessary truth that if He does, He has no cause. And it is also a necessary truth that if He has no cause, then there is no answer to a question asking for His causal conditions. The question "Why does God exist?" is, therefore, an absurdity. And in this respect there is an important analogy between the statement that God exists and any analytic statement such as "All vacuums are empty." In each case, the question "Why is it that . . . ?" cannot arise. A person who seriously asked why all vacuums are empty would betray failure to understand; in the same way someone who seriously asked why God exists would betray misapprehension of the concept of God. And this characteristic is one which the statement "God exists" or "There is a God" shares with necessary statements alone; it is in point to ask, with respect to any contingent assertion *p,* "Why is it that *p*?" That this is so may tempt one to conclude, misleadingly, that the proposition "God exists" is necessary though synthetic. This conclusion, though misleading, would serve to focus attention upon the unique role played by the assertion of God's existence in the conceptual scheme of theism. And if we bear in mind that such a conclusion could be no more than a summary way of indicating that role, perhaps no harm would result.

This account raises further questions. In particular, it leaves unexplained such notions as "dependence" and "causally necessary condition" as applied to God. And consideration of these would lead to an interesting and difficult constellation of questions regarding the Christian concepts of creation and divine omnipotence and timelessness. And so it is with any adequate explanation of any aspect of the conceptual system involved in Christianity. One aspect of it leads to and terminates in others. But to say this is only to say that the conceptual system involved in Christianity is a conceptual *system*.

3. TERENCE M. PENELHUM (1929–   )

[Terence M. Penelhum is Dean of Arts and Science
and Professor of Philosophy at the University of
Alberta, Canada. In the following essay, he considers
various conceptions of divine necessity. One should
recognize, he argues, that the question "Why does
anything exist?" is a total question; that is to say,
there is nothing missing from the question that might
be offered as an answering explanation for it. Questions of such a nature must be regarded as self-
explanatory and precisely for this reason open to objection. Self-explanatory being, for example, is a
logically impossible notion because there is no way in
which the existence of such a being could be explained
by reference to the being itself. Unfortunately, this
self-explanatory thesis is the basis of Theism's argument from causal necessity.]

Divine Necessity*

This paper is a discussion of certain limited aspects
of traditional theological doctrines of the necessity
of the divine existence and attributes. In spite of being greatly indebted to a number of recent treatments
of these themes, I still feel that something worth while
remains to be said about them, and that certain important morals can be drawn from them regarding the

* From *Mind*, Vol. LXIX (1960). Reprinted by permission
of the author and the editor of *Mind*.

relation of theistic belief to metaphysics and philosophical analysis. The traditional doctrines seem to me to be a paradigm case of the impossibility of presenting basic religious assertions as answers to metaphysical demands for explanation; but when the demonstrative trappings are carefully stripped away, what remains is seen to be of the very essence of theism, and any difficulties inherent in it are distinct from those associated with traditional attempts to *demonstrate* theism.

I shall be concerned throughout with general and not historical considerations; but those illustrative references I shall make will all be taken from the Thomistic system, since this is the most enduring and meticulous example of the doctrines I discuss, and is in one way or another normative for a great many religious thinkers. It is also considered by many to be the most modest in its metaphysical claims, but I hope to indicate that its relative agnosticism regarding the powers of the human mind does not make it less open to the criticisms to which all forms of demonstrative theism are subject.

I

Apart from the Ontological Proof, demonstrations of God's existence have taken the form of insisting that there is some fact about the world which requires explanation, and that no explanation short of a deity will do. The fact chosen will vary from thinker to thinker or chapter to chapter, but there is one clear division among those facts said to be puzzling in the way required: on the one hand there is the bare fact that there *is* a world at all, that anything exists whatever; and on the other there is the fact, or indefinitely

large group of facts, that the world is as it is, that it
contains the particular sorts of quality or relation
that it does. Since Kant there has grown up a habit
of thinking of all the demonstrations based on each
of these as just one argument, and forgetting the great
variety of arguments that have been offered of each
sort; this may not be very harmful in the first case,
but it certainly is in the second: the world is a very
varied place, and its orderliness is not the only feature
of it that has been picked out as requiring God to
explain it, even though this is the feature emphasised
in the traditional Argument from Design. To avoid any
restrictions associated with longstanding titles, I shall
talk of Existential and Qualitative arguments.

In both there are certain features of great importance:

(1) In each case the force of the argument depends
upon undermining the tendency to explain the fact
singled out by means of more normal explanatory procedures, *e.g.* scientific ones. The most effective method ·
is to render these *irrelevant* by making the puzzle too
general for ordinary procedures to solve it. In the
Existential case, temptations to explain the existence
of a given object in terms of the causal action of another are circumvented by showing that such explanations are congenitally incomplete because they leave
unanswered the general question of why anything
exists at all. In the Qualitative case, if a certain
natural feature were scientifically explained it could
be said that the natural regularity of which it was
thereby shown to be an example, or at least some
all-embracing one of which it in turn was an example,
required explanation; the fact of order itself might be
picked on for this; or one could just ask why it was

that we had the sort of world which, however naturally, gave rise to this or that feature.

(2) Although less perceptive theists have often not seen this, especially in the Qualitative case, the demands for extra-scientific explanation should logically force its users to be discontented with the mere reference to a higher being. If it is puzzling that *anything* exists, it should seem puzzling that *God* does; if a certain feature's presence in the universe is puzzling, then it should seem puzzling that it, or that which gives rise to it, should be present in God. In neither case is the explanation *complete*. To complete it more has to be built in: the being referred to has to be one whose existence, or whose possession of the relevant attributes, is self-explanatory. The potentially endless series of "Why?"-questions has to end in an answer that covers not only the last "Why?" but the next one too. So we have the doctrines of a being who necessarily *is,* or necessarily is *what* he is. It is very important to see that exactly the same theoretical move is involved whether it is said that the divine existence or nature is self-explanatory to us or merely in itself; what is essential is that the explanation should be said to lie in the divine being, even if we do not know it.

(3) As Kant saw in part, and Aquinas saw very clearly, the Qualitative question presupposes the Existential. One cannot finally answer the question of why the world is as it is without explaining why it exists, for nothing can have features unless it exists; though this is naturally only a part of the answer, since showing why anything exists is not enough to show why this sort of thing rather than that does. A theist who saw this would naturally begin by asking the Existential question, and then try to show that the being needed to answer it is implicitly enough to answer the

Qualitative. This is in part the procedure Aquinas adopts: the Existential query is clearly basic in the Five Ways, but the Qualitative is answered by implication in the discussion of the Divine Attributes, and is, I think, operative also in the Five Ways themselves.

A word here about these famous arguments. They are regularly treated, since Kant, as though they are in effect *one* argument, called The Cosmological Proof, which turns out when stated to be identical with the Third Way, or argument "from possibility and necessity." This is not confined to non-Thomists anxious to refute the arguments. E. L. Mascall, for example, says[1]

> "As I see it, the ultimate function of the Five Ways is to make it plain, by calling attention to five outstanding features of finite being, what the fundamental characteristic of finite being is. And that fundamental characteristic is its radical inability to account for its own existence."

In other words, there is at bottom only one argument: since all the beings we know are such that their existence cannot be explained by reference to them, they must derive it from outside, and ultimately from a being whose existence does not require outside explanation, and who accounts for the existence of anything whatever. This certainly fits the Second and Third Ways well enough, and perhaps the First also; and it can be made to seem a reasonable reading of the Fourth and Fifth, which involve it. But it is surely over-simple to emphasize it to the exclusion of the Qualitative query. Aquinas is surely concerned not only with the contingency of the being of finite things,

[1] E. L. Mascall, *Existence and Analogy* (New York, 1949), p. 71.

but also with that of their manner of being; in the Fourth and Fifth Ways he begins with the degrees of perfection things have and the order they exhibit, and not with their mere existence, which is more immediately his theme in the Second and Third. To borrow his language, just as the essence of finite things does not account for their existence, so the fact of their existence does not account for their essence. The ultimate answer required here is a being whose possession of the attributes necessary to cause those of finite things is self-explanatory, *i.e.* to be accounted for in terms of him. This explanation, however, would seem to have to be in terms of his existence. What else in him could his essence be explained by? So the two questions coalesce, the second vanishing into the first, perhaps, and we conclude with a being who must, by the sort of being he is, exist, and also must, by the mere fact that he exists, be the sort of being he is: one in whom essence and existence are identical. While granting Aquinas the credit for seeing that the two questions merge, and that the Existential is primary, I think it is mistaken to stress it to the extent of ignoring the presence of the Qualitative dimension from the very beginning.

II

Whether this historical excursus is sound or not, we have two archetypal questions, which seem to have clear requirements for answers, and which tend to merge.

Those who ask for them recognise that the required explanations are of quite a different order from scientific ones. We have to step out of such mundane explanatory processes and enter upon another, for they are inevitably never complete—this is the import of St. Thomas's troublesome remarks about infinite regresses. The psychological mechanism of this transition is easy to share in, but its rationality is dubious from the start, just because the kind of process we step into is of such a different order from the one we step out of. For this same reason it cannot be regarded as the completion of the ordinary explanatory processes. This is easy to see when we reflect that the only reasons for stepping out of them into it, say, six finite causes back in the series rather than sixteen or six hundred are impatience or fatigue. Philosophers, contrary to common opinion, are prone to both, but they should not found arguments upon them. In the sense in which a Necessary Being explains, contingent causes do not explain incompletely, but are not attempts to explain at all. Sceptics might say that since the concept of explanation is formed by reference to contingent causes, the demands for explanation made in our questions are spurious; a question does not become intelligible merely because of the co-presence of a curiosity-feeling.

To this the metaphysical theist might reply that it is the spuriousness, and not the genuineness, of a question that needs demonstrating, and that in the present case it is possible to explain quite clearly what sort of answer would satisfy the questioner. I would be the first to agree that when both sides insist that they are dealing with a unique case, considerations based upon this fact cannot be more than persuasive. But we do not need to rest content with these; nor do we need to consider the perplexing problem of whether there can be a question to which, in fact, there just is not

any answer;[2] we need merely to assert that there can
be no genuine question where the only possible answer
to the purported one is demonstrably absurd. And
both the Existential and the Qualitative questions
are like this.

III (a)

"Why does anything exist?" is a total question.
There can be nothing not mentioned in the question
to bring in to explain what is mentioned in the question. There are therefore three possible ways of answering it. We could say that every individual thing is
self-explanatory; we could say that the totality of
things is self-explanatory, and individuals explicable
by reference to it; or we could say that one part of
what exists is self-explanatory, and the rest explicable
by reference to that part. Of these three only the last
is of interest, since all three make use of the same
crucial concept of a self-explanatory being, and the
first two have extra problems of their own beside this.
The objection to this form of argument centres on the
self-explanatory being. Kant held that the argument
from contingent to necessary being in the Cosmological Proof reduced that argument to the Ontological
Proof, and in spite of the fact that he located this reduction in the wrong place,[3] his claim is correct.

First, what is wrong with the Ontological Proof? It
amounts to the claim that "God exists" is an analytic
proposition. The standard, and correct, objection to
this is that which Kant raised, *viz.* that to assert the

[2] R. L. Franklin, "Necessary Being," *Australasian Journal
of Philosophy* (August 1957).
[3] J. J. C. Smart, "The Existence of God," *New Essays in
Philosophical Theology,* edited by A. Flew and A. MacIntyre
(London, 1955).

existence of something is quite different from asserting what *sort* of thing it is, and to know that either
assertion is true is not to know the other is. If someone
came in unannounced and said, "It's blue!" we should
not have much idea what he was talking about, but we
would automatically know it was a visible physical object and not a philosophical theory or an Act of Parlia-
ment. But if he had come in and said "It exists!" we
should know *nothing* about what sort of thing it was.
Existence cannot vary in quantity or intensity, belong
to some members of a class and not others, or be in-
terrupted and then resumed.[4] Moore has brought out
some of the peculiarities of the word "exist" in a very
well-known paper.[5] From all this it follows that existence cannot be held to be a quality which a perfect
being would have to have, since it is not a quality at
all. So it further follows that no existential assertion
can be analytic.

So much for the Ontological Proof. It is important
to see that what refutes it is not a discovery about the
structure of things, which might in a given case be
different, but a logical discovery about the concept of
existence, which sets it apart from other concepts; that
no tautology can be existential is a consequence of
this. Another consequence is the refutation of our
Existential argument. For the distinctive character of
the concept of existence precludes our saying there
can be a being whose existence follows from his essence; and also precludes the even stronger logical
move of *identifying* the existence of anything with its
essence. These are the Anselmian error all over again.
The only other way of explaining God's existence by

[4] *Analysis*, Competition No. 11 (June 1957).
[5] G. E. Moore, "Is Existence a Predicate?" *Logic and Language*, 2d series edited by Flew (Oxford, 1953).

his essence would be by asserting a causal relationship between them, but this would run us into absurdities like saying that God would have to pre-exist himself, or that his essence would have to have something almost, but not quite, amounting to existence in order subsequently to express itself in being.

So there is no way in which the existence of *any* being could be held to be a fact explicable by reference to that being itself. Before passing to the Qualitative argument, there are two important side-issues to discuss. One is the argument of G. E. Hughes[6] that "God exists," though not analytic, might still be necessary, *i.e.* synthetically necessary; the other is the important historical claim that the Thomistic position is further removed from the Ontological Proof than any position I have considered, and is therefore unaffected by what I have said.

(i) To say that "God exists" is synthetically necessary is to run counter to fashionable views about necessity in propositions, but, as Hughes insists, one can be out of fashion and right. The difficulty for our present purpose is the notorious one for believers in synthetic necessity, of *explaining* the necessary character of the examples offered. If all necessary propositions are tautologies, this explains *why* we cannot deny them; failing an equivalent explanation, purported cases of synthetic necessity seem to have a merely subjective certainty. I do not see what sort of explanation could be had in the present case: certainly a Kantian type of explanation is unsuitable.

(ii) Since Aquinas differs from Anselm in holding that God's existence has to be inferred from his effects

---

[6] J. N. Findlay, G. E. Hughes, and A. C. A. Rainer, "Can God's Existence Be Disproved?" *New Essays in Philosophical Theology.*

and not from the mere concept of God, he is traditionally credited with having seen what was wrong with the Ontological Proof. He did see it was wrong, but not *why* it was, for he commits the same error himself. He says that we do not have the requisite knowledge of the divine nature to deduce God's existence from it; but his own argument leads us from finite beings to a being whose existence does follow from his nature, and this entails that *if* we knew God's nature we *could* deduce his existence from it—and *this* is the mistake. To say that although God's existence is self-evident in itself it is not to us is to say that it *is* self-evident in itself, and the error lies here. It is not our ignorance that is the obstacle to explaining God's existence by his nature, but the logical character of the concept of existence.

In order to introduce the morals I wish to draw from this, I shall discuss briefly a recently-expressed view of Necessary Being put forward as the basis of discussion by R. L. Franklin.[7] This is that a Necessary Being is just a being in whom the question "Why?" stops, a being about whom it makes no sense to ask it. This looks to claim less than the Thomistic position, and Franklin claims that it offers an intelligible answer to the question of why anything exists, but not a demonstrable one. It is instructive to see why this is unsatisfactory: if we cannot ask why a given being exists there must be a reason why we cannot; if there were no reason, then we *could* ask this question—such at least is the assumption made in the initial stages of any version of the Existential argument. There are two possible reasons. The first is that the being in question is self-explanatory, which I have

[7] R. L. Franklin, "Necessary Being," *Australasian Journal of Philosophy* (August 1957).

already tried to show to be an absurd reason. The second is that although the being in question is the cause of all other beings, there is no other being to be found which is the cause of *it*. In this case there would be one unexplained being, by hypothesis, and it would not answer the question of why *anything* existed. Franklin says that "Why does anything exist?" may not have an answer, but that if it does a Necessary Being (in his sense) would provide it. But a Necessary Being in his sense would not provide it, unless we went on to make it a self-explanatory being and thus reduced it to absurdity. It is not that something could provide an answer to the Existential question but maybe nothing does, but that nothing *could*.

Now for the morals:

(i) It is absurd to ask why anything exists, because the only possible answers are in terms of the logically *im*possible notion of a self-explanatory being. This is still logically impossible when it is softened by its user's saying that we personally do not know the explanation.

(ii) This in itself does not prevent us from saying that the existence of everything in the universe *except one* is due to that one (though we would presumably believe in that one for reasons not related to our present argument). But it does prevent us from going on to ask why that one exists, for *in this context* that would be *equivalent* to asking why *anything* does.

(iii) But unless you assume independently that a given being has no cause, you always can ask why it exists, *i.e.* what caused it. If you do assume it has no cause, you *ipso facto* make it impossible to ask why it is there.

(iv) So there *may* be a being who is the cause of everything else, but if there is he cannot explain the baffling fact of existence. For it is logically impossible to explain *everything*. The Principle of Sufficient Reason is demonstrably false.

(v) So the fact that things exist cannot entail the existence of God; it could only do so if God were self-explanatory. Failing this, the "Why?"-questions would only come to a halt if we had independent reasons for holding that the being we had reached was uncaused. And it would be these independent reasons that would bring us to theism. And it would not be a theism that *explained*. Theism cannot explain any more than atheism can.

III (*b*)

We turn now more briefly to our Qualitative question. The search for the complete explanation of the presence in the universe of any property is bound to lead to the claim that there is a being who has it, or some higher cause or analogate of it,[8] self-explanatorily. The objections in this case are similar:

(1) Let us call the property P. Our doctrine could mean that God has P because of some other properties he has, the relationship being causal. This clearly only pushes the problem back to these other properties themselves.

(2) The doctrine could mean "God has P" is a necessary proposition. I will assume this to mean "analytically necessary," since, as before, its being synthetically necessary might give it certitude, but not explanatory power. Now to say that "God has P" is analytic does not solve our problem, which is that of accounting for the occurrence, in the whole realm of

[8] This qualifying phrase will be assumed, but not stated, in what follows.

being, of P. If it is analytic that God has P, this just tells us that having P is part of what is meant by the word "God," *i.e.* that no being would be accorded the title who lacked P. But this merely means that there is a connection between the *concepts* of divinity and P-hood, not why either the first or the second has instances (or even *whether* either has). To know that "Birds have wings" is analytic is to know something important about the words "bird" and "wing", but nothing at all about why winged creatures came to be.

The analyticity of statements about God has been thought to raise more problems than it does. C. B. Martin[9] has claimed that since "God is good" is analytic, God cannot be identified with the man Jesus, for "Jesus is good" is synthetic. This can be resolved by using Martin's own distinction between "God" as a proper name, and "God" as a *concept*.[10] "God(concept) is good" is analytic; but "God(proper name) is good" is synthetic, and learned, if at all, by experience. In our present case the problem posed by the Qualitative query is that of explaining the fact reported by "God(proper name) has P." This is not explained by showing that "God(concept) has P" is analytic, even though it is.

(3) Only one recourse remains. Since the divine possession of P cannot be explained by reference to the divine nature, it can only be explained by reference to the divine existence. Let us say, then, that God's having P is a deducible consequence of the fact of his existence. This would only explain his having P if his existence were previously said to be necessary, but let

[9] C. B. Martin, "The Perfect Good," *New Essays in Philosophical Theology.*

[10] Alan Donagan, *Review of New Essays in Philosophical Theology,* in *Philosophical Review* (July 1957).

us ignore this. What is said of P would apply, by parity of reasoning, to all the divine attributes; so we come once more to the identity of the divine essence and existence, with some kind of priority being accorded to the divine existence. The connection between the Existential and Qualitative arguments is closer than Kant recognised.

The objections are not hard to find:

(i) Quite apart from the difficulties involved in saying God necessarily exists, we have gone in a circle if we fall back on this here. For we began by explaining his existence in terms of his essence, and we now find ourselves explaining his essence in terms of his existence.

(ii) The logical character of the concept of existence is not only enough to render it inadmissible to infer God's existence from his essence, but also renders it inadmissible to infer his essence from his existence—or, again, to identify them.

The morals to be drawn are the same:

(i) It is absurd to ask why anything has P, for the only possible answers are in terms of the logically *impossible* notion of a being in whom the presence of P is self-explanatory, etc.

(ii) This in itself does not prevent us from saying that the presence of P in any being in the universe *except one* is due to its presence in that one, etc. But it does prevent us from going on to ask why that being has P, for *in this context* that would be *equivalent* to asking why *anything* does.

(iii) But unless you assume independently that a given being has P without cause, you can always ask why it has P, etc.

(iv) So there *may* be a being who is the cause of

all *other* beings' having P who have it, but he cannot explain the baffling fact of P itself, etc.

(v) So the fact that P can be found cannot entail that there is a God who has P; it could only do so if God's having P were self-explanatory. Failing this, the "Why P?"-questions would only come to a halt if we had independent reasons for holding that the being we had reached had P without cause, etc.

IV

There can, then, be no metaphysical compulsion to believe in God; for the sort of metaphysical questions which would necessitate theism are spurious. This does not refute theism, however. It would only refute it if the sort of explanatory demand we have been considering were inevitably involved in belief in God. This has been argued by J. N. Findlay;[11] he says that the attitude of worship entails God's complete independence of all other beings, both in his existence and his possession of his excellences, and entails that he possesses these in the highest conceivable degree; if this is accepted, and it seems it must be, he claims we have to go on to say that God exists and has his excellences in some necessary manner; given the absurdity of this, God's non-existence follows.

Theism can be rescued from his argument. One can agree with Aquinas that it is no limitation on God that he cannot perform logical absurdities; and one can adapt this and say it is no limitation on him that he

[11] J. N. Findlay, G. E. Hughes, and A. C. A. Rainer, "Can God's Existence be Disproved?" *New Essays in Philosophical Theology.*

cannot *be* a logical absurdity; and that is what a Necessary Being, *in the sense we have examined,* is. I think the readiness of Findlay's disputants to agree that God's existence and excellence are necessary is due to a dangerous and crucial ambiguity in the terms "necessary" and "contingent" (an ambiguity almost, but not quite, recognised by Rainer). It is pedantic of philosophers to insist that these words only apply to propositions and not to things; but our previous discussion should show that they will mean something different in each case. We do not need to say precisely here what propositional necessity is: let us say that, roughly, a proposition is necessary if its truth can be known without reference to anything other than a clear understanding of what is said or implied in it; contingency in propositions is the absence of necessity (and of its contrary, *viz.* necessary falsehood or, if this is the same, self-contradiction). As applied to things or events, "contingent" will mean "dependent" or "caused," one thing or event being contingent *upon* another; "necessary" will mean "not dependent on any other," and, in addition, "having others dependent on it." A thing is necessary if it is indispensable. For want of a better phrase I shall call necessity in this sense "factual necessity." To be a theist is to believe that there is a being, God, who is factually necessary, all other beings being dependent, contingent, upon him. But the *assertion* of this will be a contingent assertion, in the propositional sense (and not in the Thomistic sense that Rainer adopts, viz. contingent to us but necessary for God). God's existence and nature are unique in the universe in being free of factual contingency, but the assertions of them share in propositional contingency with all other assertions of fact.

Theists believe that God exists, that he is supremely great and good, that no other beings would exist if he did not, and that all their multitudinous features have their source in him. I have denied none of this. It merely means that God is factually necessary, indispensable. I have denied he can be necessary in any other sense, that he explains either his own existence or nature, or, ultimately, that of other things. Since this ideal is bogus, God is not denigrated if he is not held to realise it. If there is a factually necessary being then, this fact, though the most important fact there is, could not be proved.

"Why, then, be a Theist?" Well, theism is older than the Cosmological Proof, and can survive it. Some have tried to present it as an ordinary empirical hypothesis, but this has seldom impressed. If theism is to be seen to be true at all, it looks as though this will have to happen through individual confrontation with what purports to be God's self-revelation. A person who accepts this and then proclaims it to others is not free from philosophical criticism just because he does not proclaim his belief as metaphysically necessary; for he still makes statements which do not always appear to others to have the relationship to evidence which all statements (they say) have to have; and if "metaphysics" is defined in the required way, what he says will be metaphysical to them still. But the objections thus raised against theism when it is expressed in undemonstrated assertions by such a person, however strong they are, are distinct from those much stronger ones that can be brought against offering theism as the answer to the sort of confused question we have examined above; and the sort of "metaphysics" that may be contained in them or spun around them is likely to be immune to the objections we have stressed, whatever its other defects may be. Philosophical analysis will not progress much in understanding religious assertions, especially their relationship to metaphysical speculation, unless these distinctions are carefully borne in mind.

PART II

THE TELEOLOGICAL ARGUMENT

A. THE CLASSICAL VIEW

1. WILLIAM PALEY (1743–1805)

[William Paley, Archdeacon of Carlisle, was notable both as Christian apologist and as instructor in moral philosophy. His fame as apologist and philosopher stems primarily from three works: *Principles of Moral and Political Philosophy* (1785), *View of the Evidences of Christianity* (1794), and *Natural Theology, or Evidences of the Existence and Attributes of the Deity Collected from the Appearances of Nature* (1802). Each work has gone through numerous editions. The familiar argument based on "watch and watchmaker" appears on the following pages. It is noteworthy that the same analogy was suggested by Voltaire.]

The Attributes of Deity from the Appearances of Nature*

STATE OF THE ARGUMENT

In crossing a heath, suppose I pitched my foot against a *stone,* and were asked how the stone came to be there; I might possibly answer, that, for any thing I knew to the contrary, it had lain there for ever: nor would it perhaps be very easy to show the absurdity of this answer. But suppose I had found a *watch* upon

* From *Paley's Works* (London 1842). *Natural Theology,* Chapter I.

the ground, and it should be inquired how the watch happened to be in that place; I should hardly think of the answer which I had before given, that, for any thing I knew, the watch might have always been there. Yet why should not this answer serve for the watch as well as for the stone? why is it not as admissible in the second case, as in the first? For this reason, and for no other, viz. that, when we come to inspect the watch, we perceive (what we could not discover in the stone) that its several parts are framed and put together for a purpose, *e. g.* that they are so formed and adjusted as to produce motion, and that motion so regulated as to point out the hour of the day; that, if the different parts had been differently shaped from what they are, of a different size from what they are, or placed after any other manner, or in any other order, than that in which they are placed, either no motion at all would have been carried on in the machine, or none which would have answered the use that is now served by it. To reckon up a few of the plainest of these parts, and of their offices, all tending to one result:—We see a cylindrical box containing a coiled elastic spring, which, by its endeavour to relax itself, turns round the box. We next observe a flexible chain (artificially wrought for the sake of flexure), communicating the action of the spring from the box to the fusee. We then find a series of wheels, the teeth of which catch in, and apply to each other, conducting the motion from the fusee to the balance, and from the balance to the pointer; and at the same time, by the size and shape of those wheels, so regulating that motion, as to terminate in causing an index, by an equable and measured progression, to pass over a given space in a given time. We take notice that the wheels are made of brass in order to keep them from rust; the springs of steel, no other metal being so elastic; that over the face of the watch there is placed a glass, a material employed in no other part of the work, but in the room of which, if there had been any other than a transparent substance, the hour could not be seen without opening the case. This mechanism being observed (it requires indeed an examination of the instrument, and perhaps some previous knowledge of the subject, to perceive and understand it; but being once, as we have said, observed and understood), the inference, we think, is inevitable, that the watch must have had a maker; that there must have existed, at some time, and at some place or other, an artificer or artificers, who formed it for the purpose which we find it actually to answer; who comprehended its construction, and designed its use.

I. Nor would it, I apprehend, weaken the conclusion, that we had never seen a watch made; that we had never known an artist capable of making one; that we were altogether incapable of executing such a piece of workmanship ourselves, or of understanding in what manner it was performed; all this being no more than what is true of some exquisite remains of ancient art, of some lost arts, and, to the generality of mankind, of the more curious productions of modern manufacture. Does one man in a million know how oval frames are turned? Ignorance of this kind exalts our opinion of the unseen and unknown artist's skill, if he be unseen and unknown, but raises no doubt in our minds of the existence and agency of such an artist, at some former time, and in some place or other. Nor can I perceive that it varies at all the inference, whether the question arise concerning a human agent, or concerning an agent of a different species, or an agent possessing, in some respects, a different nature.

II. Neither, secondly, would it invalidate our conclusion, that the watch sometimes went wrong, or that it seldom went exactly right. The purpose of the machinery, the design, and the designer, might be evident, and in the case supposed would be evident, in whatever way we accounted for the irregularity of the movement, or whether we could account for it or not. It is not necessary that a machine be perfect, in order to show with what design it was made; still less necessary, where the only question is, whether it were made with any design at all.

III. Nor, thirdly, would it bring any uncertainty into the argument, if there were a few parts of the watch, concerning which we could not discover, or had not yet discovered, in what manner they conduced to the general effect; or even some parts, concerning which we could not ascertain, whether they conduced to that effect in any manner whatever. For, as to the first branch of the case; if by the loss, or disorder, or decay of the parts in question, the movement of the watch were found in fact to be stopped, or disturbed, or retarded, no doubt would remain in our minds as to the utility or intention of these parts, although we should be unable to investigate the manner according to which, or the connection by which, the ultimate effect depended upon their action or assistance; and the more complex is the machine, the more likely is this obscurity to arise. Then, as to the second thing supposed, namely, that there were parts which might be spared, without prejudice to the movement of the watch, and that we had proved this by experiment,— these superfluous parts, even if we were completely assured that they were such, would not vacate the reasoning which we had instituted concerning other parts.

The indication of contrivance remained, with respect to them, nearly as it was before.

IV. Nor, fourthly, would any man in his senses think the existence of the watch, with its various machinery, accounted for, by being told that it was one out of possible combinations of material forms; that whatever he had found in the place where he found the watch, must have contained some internal configuration or other; and that this configuration might be the structure now exhibited, viz. of the works of a watch, as well as a different structure.

V. Nor, fifthly, would it yield his inquiry more satisfaction to be answered, that there existed in things a principle of order, which had disposed the parts of the watch into their present form and situation. He never knew a watch made by the principle of order; nor can he even form to himself an idea of what is meant by a principle of order, distinct from the intelligence of the watchmaker.

VI. Sixthly, he would be surprised to hear that the mechanism of the watch was no proof of contrivance, only a motive to induce the mind to think so.

VII. And not less surprised to be informed, that the watch in his hand was nothing more than the result of the laws of *metallic* nature. It is a perversion of language to assign any law, as the efficient, operative cause of any thing. A law presupposes an agent; for it is only the mode, according to which an agent proceeds: it implies a power; for it is the order, according to which that power acts. Without this agent, without this power, which are both distinct from itself, the *law* does nothing; is nothing. The expression, "the law of metallic nature," may sound strange and harsh to a philosophic ear; but it seems quite as justifiable as some others which are more familiar to him, such as "the law of vegetable nature," "the law of animal nature," or indeed as "the law of nature," in general, when assigned as the cause of phenomena, in exclusion of agency and power; or when it is substituted into the place of these.

VIII. Neither, lastly, would our observer be driven out of his conclusion, or from his confidence in its truth, by being told that he knew nothing at all about the matter. He knows enough for his argument: he knows the utility of the end: he knows the subserviency and adaptation of the means to the end. These points being known, his ignorance of other points, his doubts concerning other points, affect not the certainty of his reasoning. The consciousness of knowing little, need not beget a distrust of that which he does know.

The conclusion which the . . . examination of the watch, of its works, construction, and movement, suggested, was, that it must have had, for the cause and author of that construction, an artificer, who understood its mechanism, and designed its use. This conclusion is invincible. . . . [And]: for every indication of contrivance, every manifestation of design, which existed in the watch, exists in the works of nature; with the difference, on the side of nature, of being greater and more, and that in a degree which exceeds all computation. I mean, that the contrivances of nature surpass the contrivances of art, in the complexity, subtility, and curiosity of the mechanism; and still more, if possible, do they go beyond them in number and variety; yet, in a multitude of cases, are not less evidently mechanical, not less evidently contrivances, not less evidently accommodated to their end, or suited to their office, than are the most perfect productions of human ingenuity.

2. DAVID HUME

[It may seem strange, that defense of the teleological argument is undertaken in the following by one who apparently had little sympathy with it. However, it only emphasizes Hume's great philosophical ingenuity, for he does not shirk the task of putting the argument forceably. Furthermore, it is noteworthy that Hume is not completely convinced that the argument is vitiated even by his own criticism. In the penultimate paragraph of the *Dialogues* the skeptic Philo says, "The cause or causes of order in the universe probably bear some remote analogy to human intelligence." But it remains for Cleanthes to present the argument, maintaining that there are adequate *a posteriori* reasons for accepting the premise that a Deity exists. Because the world is one vast machine and is divisible into a network of smaller and yet comparable machines that far outstrip human comprehension, reasonable men, he says, are forced to conclude that the source of everything is a superior mind or intelligence.]

Cleanthes' Argument from Design*

Not to lose any time in circumlocutions, said Cleanthes, addressing himself to Demea, much less in replying to the pious declamations of Philo; I shall briefly

* From *Dialogues Concerning Natural Religion*. Selections from Parts II, III, IV. *The Philosophical Works of David Hume* (Boston, 1854).

explain how I conceive this matter. Look round the world: contemplate the whole and every part of it: you will find it to be nothing but one great machine, subdivided into an infinite number of lesser machines, which again admit of subdivisions to a degree beyond what human senses and faculties can trace and explain. All these various machines, and even their most minute parts, are adjusted to each other with an accuracy which ravishes into admiration all men who have ever contemplated them. The curious adapting of means to ends, throughout all nature, resembles exactly, though it much exceeds, the productions of human contrivance; of human designs, thought, wisdom, and intelligence. Since, therefore, the effects resemble each other, we are led to infer, by all the rules of analogy, that the causes also resemble; and that the Author of Nature is somewhat similar to the mind of man, though possessed of much larger faculties, proportioned to the grandeur of the work which he has executed. By this argument *a posteriori,* and by this argument alone, do we prove at once the existence of a Deity, and his similarity to human mind and intelligence. . . .

Suppose . . . that an articulate voice were heard in the clouds, much louder and more melodious than any which human art could ever reach: suppose, that this voice were extended in the same instant over all nations, and spoke to each nation in its own language and dialect: suppose, that the words delivered not only contain a just sense and meaning, but convey some instruction altogether worthy of a benevolent Being, superior to mankind: could you possibly hesitate a moment concerning the cause of this voice? and must you not instantly ascribe it to some design or purpose? Yet I cannot see but all the same objections (if they merit that appellation) which lie against the system of The-ism, may also be produced against this inference.

Might you not say, that all conclusions concerning fact were founded on experience: that when we hear an articulate voice in the dark, and thence infer a man, it is only the resemblance of the effects which leads us to conclude that there is a like resemblance in the cause: but that this extraordinary voice, by its loud-ness, extent, and flexibility to all languages, bears so little analogy to any human voice, that we have no rea-son to suppose any analogy in their causes: and con-sequently, that a rational, wise, coherent speech pro-ceeded, you know not whence, from some accidental whistling of the winds, not from any divine reason or intelligence? You see clearly your own objections in these cavils, and I hope too you see clearly, that they cannot possibly have more force in the one case than in the other.

But to bring the case still nearer the present one of the universe, I shall make two suppositions, which im-ply not any absurdity or impossibility. Suppose that there is a natural, universal, invariable language, com-mon to every individual of human race; and that books are natural productions, which perpetuate themselves in the same manner with animals and vegetables, by descent and propagation. Several expressions of our passions contain a universal language: all brute ani-mals have a natural speech, which, however limited, is very intelligible to their own species. And as there are infinitely fewer parts and less contrivance in the finest composition of eloquence, than in the coarsest organized body, the propagation of an Iliad or Æneid is an easier supposition than that of any plant or animal.

Suppose, therefore, that you enter into your library,

thus peopled by natural volumes, containing the most refined reason and most exquisite beauty; could you possibly open one of them, and doubt, that its original cause bore the strongest analogy to mind and intelligence? When it reasons and discourses; when it expostulates, argues, and enforces its views and topics; when it applies sometimes to the pure intellect, sometimes to the affections; when it collects, disposes, and adorns every consideration suited to the subject; could you persist in asserting, that all this, at the bottom, had really no meaning; and that the first formation of this volume in the loins of its original parent proceeded not from thought and design? Your obstinacy, I know, reaches not that degree of firmness: even your sceptical play and wantonness would be abashed at so glaring an absurdity.

But if there be any difference, Philo, between this supposed case and the real one of the universe, it is all to the advantage of the latter. The anatomy of an animal affords many stronger instances of design than the perusal of Livy or Tacitus; and any objection which you start in the former case, by carrying me back to so unusual and extraordinary a scene as the first formation of worlds, the same objection has place on the supposition of our vegetating library. Choose, then, your party, Philo, without ambiguity or evasion; assert either that a rational volume is no proof of a rational cause, or admit of a similar cause to all the works of nature.

Let me here observe too, continued Cleanthes, that this religious argument, instead of being weakened by that scepticism so much affected by you, rather acquires force from it, and becomes more firm and undisputed. To exclude all argument or reasoning of every kind, is either affectation or madness. The declared profession of every reasonable sceptic is only to reject abstruse, remote, and refined arguments; to adhere to common sense and the plain instincts of nature; and to assent, wherever any reasons strike him with so full a force that he cannot, without the greatest violence, prevent it. Now the arguments for Natural Religion are plainly of this kind; and nothing but the most perverse, obstinate metaphysics can reject them. Consider, anatomize the eye; survey its structure and contrivance; and tell me, from your own feeling, if the idea of a contriver does not immediately flow in upon you with a force like that of sensation. The most obvious conclusion, surely, is in favor of design; and it requires time, reflection, and study, to summon up those frivolous, though abstruse objections, which can support Infidelity. Who can behold the male and female of each species, the correspondence of their parts and instincts, their passions, and whole course of life before and after generation, but must be sensible, that the propagation of the species is intended by Nature? Millions and millions of such instances present themselves through every part of the universe; and no language can convey a more intelligible irresistible meaning, than the curious adjustment of final causes. To what degree, therefore, of blind dogmatism must one have attained, to reject such natural and such convincing arguments?

Some beauties in writing we may meet with, which seem contrary to rules, and which gain the affections, and animate the imagination, in opposition to all the precepts of criticism, and to the authority of the established masters of art. And if the argument for Theism be, as you pretend, contradictory to the principles of logic; its universal, its irresistible influence proves clearly, that there may be arguments of a like irregular nature. Whatever cavils may be urged, an orderly world, as well as a coherent, articulate speech, will still be received as an incontestable proof of design and intention.

It sometimes happens, I own, that the religious arguments have not their due influence on an ignorant savage and barbarian; not because they are obscure and difficult, but because he never asks himself any question with regard to them. Whence arises the curious structure of an animal? From the copulation of its parents. And these whence? From *their* parents? A few removes set the objects at such a distance, that to him they are lost in darkness and confusion; nor is he actuated by any curiosity to trace them further. But this is neither dogmatism nor scepticism, but stupidity: a state of mind very different from your sifting, inquisitive disposition, my ingenious friend. You can trace causes from effects: you can compare the most distant and remote objects: and your greatest errors proceed not from barrenness of thought and invention, but from too luxuriant a fertility, which suppresses your natural good sense, by a profusion of unnecessary scruples and objections. . . .

The order and arrangement of nature, the curious adjustment of final causes, the plain use and intention of every part and organ; all these bespeak in the clearest language an intelligent cause or author. The heavens and the earth join in the same testimony: the whole chorus of Nature raises one hymn to the praises of its Creator. You alone, or almost alone, disturb this general harmony. You start abstruse doubts, cavils, and objections: you ask me, what is the cause of this cause? I know not; I care not; that concerns not me. I have found a Deity; and here I stop my inquiry. Let those go further, who are wiser or more enterprising.

3. JOHN STUART MILL (1806–73)

[Charles Darwin's *Origin of Species* appeared in 1859 and John Stuart Mill's *Nature and Utility of Religion* was published in 1874. It is interesting to notice the ambivalence with which Mill responds to the Darwinian thesis. He acknowledges that the "survival of the fittest" principle may account for the state of nature, but he does not believe that this is incompatible with creationism. He is not convinced that "natural selection" provides sufficient explanation for nature's teleological structure, which not only supports the so-called "watch and watchmaker" analogue as Paley had argued but is also inductively impelling. It is the inductive quality of the teleological argument that insulates Mill from the full force of Darwin's hypothesis. The impartial observer, Mill maintains, is either required to accept the thesis that there is, so to speak, "behind" nature a master intelligence that directs things, or forced to conclude that nature, from its primeval beginnings to its present complex state, has passed through numerous stages of development that are merely accidental—a position that seems not nearly as incredible now, of course, as it did to Mill.]

Marks of Design in Nature*

We now at last reach an argument of a really scientific character, which does not shrink from scientific

* From *Three Essays on Religion: Nature, the Utility of Religion, and Theism* (New York, 1874).

tests, but claims to be judged by the established canons of Induction. The Design argument is wholly grounded on experience. Certain qualities, it is alleged, are found to be characteristic of such things as are made by an intelligent mind for a purpose. The order of Nature, or some considerable parts of it, exhibit these qualities in a remarkable degree. We are entitled, from this great similarity in the effects, to infer similarity in the cause, and to believe that things which it is beyond the power of man to make, but which resemble the works of man in all but power, must also have been made by Intelligence, armed with a power greater than human.

I have stated this argument in its fullest strength, as it is stated by its most thoroughgoing assertors. A very little consideration, however, suffices to show that though it has some force, its force is very generally overrated. Paley's illustration of a watch puts the case much too strongly. If I found a watch on an apparently desolate island, I should indeed infer that it had been left there by a human being; but the inference would not be from marks of design, but because I already knew by direct experience that watches are made by men. I should draw the inference no less confidently from a foot print, or from any relic however insignificant which experience has taught me to attribute to man: as geologists infer the past existence of animals from coprolites,[1] though no one sees marks of design in a coprolite. The evidence of design in creation can never reach the height of direct induction; it amounts only to the inferior kind of inductive evidence called analogy. Analogy agrees with induction in this, that they both argue that a thing known to resemble

[1] Fossil dung.

another in certain circumstances (call those circumstances A and B) will resemble it in another circumstance (call it C). But the difference is that in induction, A and B are known, by a previous comparison of many instances, to be the very circumstances on which C depends, or with which it is in some way connected. When this has not been ascertained, the argument amounts only to this, that since it is not known with which of the circumstances existing in the known case C is connected, they may as well be A and B as any others; and therefore there is a greater probability of C in cases where we know that A and B exist, than in cases of which we know nothing at all. This argument is of a weight very difficult to estimate at all, and impossible to estimate precisely. It may be very strong, when the known points of agreement, A and B &c. are numerous and the known points of difference few; or very weak, when the reverse is the case: but it can never be equal in validity to a real induction. The resemblances between some of the arrangements in nature and some of those made by man are considerable, and even as mere resemblances afford a certain presumption of similarity of cause: but how great that presumption is, it is hard to say. All that can be said with certainty is that these likenesses make creation by intelligence considerably more probable than if the likenesses had been less, or than if there had been no likenesses at all.

This mode, however, of stating the case does not do full justice to the evidence of Theism. The Design argument is not drawn from mere resemblances in Nature to the works of human intelligence, but from the special character of those resemblances. The circumstances in which it is alleged that the world resembles the works of man are not circumstances taken at random, but are particular instances of a circumstance which experience shows to have a real connection with an intelligent origin, the fact of conspiring to an end. The argument therefore is not one of mere analogy. As mere analogy it has its weight, but it is more than analogy. It surpasses analogy exactly as induction surpasses it. It is an inductive argument.

This, I think, is undeniable, and it remains to test the argument by the logical principles applicable to Induction. For this purpose it will be convenient to handle, not the argument as a whole, but some one of the most impressive cases of it, such as the structure of the eye, or of the ear. It is maintained that the structure of the eye proves a designing mind. To what class of inductive arguments does this belong? and what is its degree of force?

The species of inductive arguments are four in number, corresponding to the four Inductive Methods; the Methods of Agreement, of Difference, of Residues, and of Concomitant Variations. The argument under consideration falls within the first of these divisions, the Method of Agreement. This is, for reasons known to inductive logicians, the weakest of the four, but the particular argument is a strong one of the kind. It may be logically analysed as follows:

The parts of which the eye is composed, and the collocations which constitute the arrangement of those parts, resemble one another in this very remarkable property, that they all conduce to enabling the animal to see. These things being as they are, the animal sees: if any one of them were different from what it is, the animal, for the most part, would either not see, or would not see equally well. And this is the only marked resemblance that we can trace among the different parts of this structure, beyond the general likeness of composition and organization which exists among all other parts of the animal. Now the particular combination of organic elements called an eye had, in every instance, a beginning in time and must therefore have been brought together by a cause or causes. The number of instances is immeasurably greater than is, by the principles of inductive logic, required for the exclusion of a random concurrence of independent causes, or speaking technically, for the elimination of chance. We are therefore warranted by the canons of induction in concluding that what brought all these elements together was some cause common to them all; and inasmuch as the elements agree in the single circumstance of conspiring to produce sight, there must be some connection by way of causation between the cause which brought those elements together, and the fact of sight.

This I conceive to be a legitimate inductive inference, and the sum and substance of what Induction can do for Theism. The natural sequel of the argument would be this. Sight, being a fact not precedent but subsequent to the putting together of the organic structure of the eye, can only be connected with the production of that structure in the character of a final, not an efficient cause; that is, it is not Sight itself but an antecedent Idea of it, that must be the efficient cause. But this at once marks the origin as proceeding from an intelligent will.

I regret to say, however, that this latter half of the argument is not so inexpugnable as the former half. Creative forethought is not absolutely the only link by which the origin of the wonderful mechanism of the eye may be connected with the fact of sight. There is another connecting link on which attention has been greatly fixed by recent speculations, and the reality of which cannot be called in question, though its adequacy to account for such truly admirable combinations as some of those in Nature, is still and will probably long remain problematical. This is the principle of "the survival of the fittest."

This principle does not pretend to account for the commencement of sensation or of animal or vegetable life. But assuming the existence of some one or more very low forms of organic life, in which there are no complex adaptations nor any marked appearances of contrivance, and supposing, as experience warrants us in doing, that many small variations from those simple types would be thrown out in all directions, which would be transmissible by inheritance, and of which some would be advantageous to the creature in its struggle for existence and others disadvantageous, the forms which are advantageous would always tend to survive and those which are disadvantageous to perish. And thus there would be a constant though slow general improvement of the type as it branched out into many different varieties, adapting it to different media and modes of existence, until it might possibly, in countless ages, attain to the most advanced examples which now exist.

It must be acknowledged that there is something very startling, and *prima facie* improbable in this hypothetical history of Nature. It would require us, for example, to suppose that the primæval animal of whatever nature it may have been, could not see, and had at most such slight preparation for seeing as might be constituted by some chemical action of light upon its cellular structure. One of the accidental variations which are liable to take place in all organic beings would at some time or other produce a variety that could see, in some imperfect manner, and this peculiarity being transmitted by inheritance, while other variations continued to take place in other directions, a number of races would be produced who, by the power of even imperfect sight, would have a great advantage over all other creatures which could not see and would in time extirpate them from all places, except, perhaps, a few very peculiar situations underground. Fresh variations supervening would give rise to races with better and better seeing powers until we might at last reach as extraordinary a combination of structures and functions as are seen in the eye of man and of the more important animals. Of this theory when pushed to this extreme point, all that can now be said is that it is not so absurd as it looks, and that the analogies which have been discovered in experience, favourable to its possibility, far exceed what any one could have supposed beforehand. Whether it will ever be possible to say more than this, is at present uncertain. The theory if admitted would be in no way whatever inconsistent with Creation. But it must be acknowledged that it would greatly attenuate the evidence for it.

Leaving this remarkable speculation to whatever fate the progress of discovery may have in store for it, I think it must be allowed that, in the present state of our knowledge, the adaptations in Nature afford a large balance of probability in favour of creation by intelligence. It is equally certain that this is no more than a probability; and that the various other arguments of Natural Theology which we have considered, add nothing to its force. Whatever ground there is, revelation apart, to believe in an Author of Nature, is derived from the appearances in the universe. Their mere resemblance to the works of man, or to what man could do if he had the same power over the materials of organized bodies which he has over the materials of a watch, is of some value as an argument of analogy: but the argument is greatly strengthened by the properly inductive considerations which establish that there is some connection through causation between the origin of the arrangements of nature and the ends they fulfil; an argument which is in many cases slight, but in others, and chiefly in the nice and intricate combinations of vegetable and animal life, is of considerable strength.

B. THE CLASSICAL CRITIQUE

1. DAVID HUME

[Once again it is possible to turn to the genius of Hume for expression on the issue. In this selection it is Philo who rejects the teleological anthropomorphisms of Cleanthes—arguing, first, that one cannot maintain that God is infinite because nothing in the concept of cause necessitates that it be infinite; second, that an anthropomorphic deity need not possess the attribute of perfection; and finally, that the thesis need not restrict theism to a single God as Cleanthes wishes. Clearly, the conception of God is left to man's imagination—a position hardly preferable to agnosticism. Philo maintains that things, to considerable degree, manifest design by the very fact that they have a relationship to other things. In other words, if the universe is not perceived as having one particular design, then it will be perceived as having another.]

Philo's Objections to the Arguments from Design*

But to show you still more inconveniences, continued Philo, in your Anthropomorphism, please to take a new survey of your principles. *Like effects prove like causes.* This is the experimental argument; and this, you say too, is the sole theological argument. Now, it is certain, that the liker the effects are which are seen,

* From *Dialogues Concerning Natural Religion*. Selections from Parts V, VIII. *The Philosophical Works of David Hume* (Boston, 1854).

and the liker the causes which are inferred, the stronger
is the argument. Every departure on either side dimin-
ishes the probability, and renders the experiment less
conclusive. You cannot doubt of the principle; neither
ought you to reject its consequences.

All the new discoveries in astronomy, which prove
the immense grandeur and magnificence of the works
of Nature, are so many additional arguments for a
Deity, according to the true system of Theism; but,
according to your hypothesis of experimental Theism,
they become so many objections, by removing the effect still further from all resemblance to the effects of
human art and contrivance. For, if Lucretius,[1] even
following the old system of the world, could exclaim,

> Quis regere immensi summam, quis habere profundi
> Indu manu validas potis est moderanter habenas?
> Quis pariter cœlos omnes convertere? et omnes
> Ignibus ætheriis terras suffire feraces?
> Omnibus inque locis esse omni tempore præsto?[2]

If Tully[3] esteemed this reasoning so natural, as to put
it into the mouth of his Epicurean: "Quibus enim ocu-
lis animi intueri potuit vester Plato fabricam illam
tanti operis, qua construi a Deo atque ædificari mun-
dum facit? quæ molito? quæ ferramenta? qui vectes?
quæ machinæ? qui minstri tanti muneris fuerunt?
quemadmodum autem obedire et parere voluntati ar-

---

[1] Lib. xi. 1094.
[2] Who has power to rule over all the boundless seas,
   Whose hand can hold on course the strong reins of the
   deep?
   Again, who is able to whirl the heavens about?
   to warm the fertile earth with heavenly fires?
   or to be present in all places at all times?
   (Trans. S. K. Basmajian.)
[3] *De Nat. Deor.,* lib. i [Cicero].

chitecti aer, ignis, aqua, terra potuerunt?"[4] If this argument, I say, had any force in former ages, how much greater must it have at present, when the bounds of Nature are so infinitely enlarged, and such a magnificent scene is opened to us? It is still more unreasonable to form our idea of so unlimited a cause from our experience of the narrow productions of human design and invention.

The discoveries by microscopes, as they open a new universe in miniature, are still objections, according to you, arguments, according to me. The further we push our researches of this kind, we are still led to infer the universal cause of all to be vastly different from mankind, or from any object of human experience and observation.

And what say you to the discoveries in anatomy, chemistry, botany? . . . . . These surely are no objections, replied Cleanthes; they only discover new instances of art and contrivance. It is still the image of mind reflected on us from innumerable objects. Add, a mind *like the human*, said Philo. I know of no other, replied Cleanthes. And the liker the better, insisted Philo. To be sure, said Cleanthes.

Now, Cleanthes, said Philo, with an air of alacrity and triumph, mark the consequences. *First*, By this method of reasoning, you renounce all claim to infinity in any of the attributes of the Deity. For, as the cause ought only to be proportioned to the effect, and the

[4] For with what inner eyes was your Plato able to gaze upon that splendid product of such great workmanship and say that the world was fashioned and built by God? What was the mighty effort of creation? What kind of tools, what levers, what machines were used? What servants of so high an office were there to assist? How was it, moreover, that the elemental air, fire, water, and earth could heed and perform the builder's will? (Trans. S. K. Basmajian.)

effect, so far as it falls under our cognizance, is not infinite; what pretensions have we, upon your suppositions, to ascribe that attribute to the Divine Being? You will still insist, that, by removing him so much from all similarity to human creatures, we give in to the most arbitrary hypothesis, and at the same time weaken all proofs of his existence.

Secondly, You have no reason, on your theory, for ascribing perfection to the Deity, even in his finite capacity, or for supposing him free from every error, mistake, or incoherence, in his undertakings. There are many inexplicable difficulties in the works of Nature, which, if we allow a perfect author to be proved *a priori,* are easily solved, and become only seeming difficulties, from the narrow capacity of man, who cannot trace infinite relations. But according to your method of reasoning, these difficulties become all real; and perhaps will be insisted on, as new instances of likeness to human art and contrivance. At least, you must acknowledge, that it is impossible for us to tell, from our limited views, whether this system contains any great faults, or deserves any considerable praise, if compared to other possible, and even real systems. Could a peasant, if the Æneid were read to him, pronounce that poem to be absolutely faultless, or even assign to it its proper rank among the productions of human wit, he, who had never seen any other production?

But were this world ever so perfect a production, it must still remain uncertain, whether all the excellences of the work can justly be ascribed to the workman. If we survey a ship, what an exalted idea must we form of the ingenuity of the carpenter who framed so complicated, useful, and beautiful a machine? And what surprise must we feel, when we find him a stupid mechanic, who imitated others, and copied an art, which, through a long succession of ages, after multiplied trials, mistakes, corrections, deliberations, and controversies, had been gradually improving? Many worlds might have been botched and bungled, throughout an eternity, ere this system was struck out; much labor lost, many fruitless trials made; and a slow, but continued improvement carried on during infinite ages in the art of world-making. In such subjects, who can determine, where the truth; nay, who can conjecture where the probability lies, amidst a great number of hypotheses which may be proposed, and a still greater which may be imagined?

And what shadow of an argument, continued Philo, can you produce, from your hypothesis, to prove the unity of the Deity? A great number of men join in building a house or ship, in rearing a city, in framing a commonwealth; why may not several deities combine in contriving and framing a world? This is only so much greater similarity to human affairs. By sharing the work among several, we may so much further limit the attributes of each, and get rid of that extensive power and knowledge, which must be supposed in one deity, and which, according to you, can only serve to weaken the proof of his existence. And if such foolish, such vicious creatures as man, can yet often unite in framing and executing one plan, how much more those deities or demons, whom we may suppose several degrees more perfect!

To multiply causes without necessity, is indeed contrary to true philosophy: but this principle applies not to the present case. Were one deity antecedently proved by your theory, who were possessed of every attribute requisite to the production of the universe; it would be needless, I own, (though not absurd,) to suppose any other deity existent. But while it is still a question, Whether all these attributes are united in one subject, or dispersed among several independent beings, by what phenomena in nature can we pretend to decide the controversy? Where we see a body raised in a scale, we are sure that there is in the opposite scale, however concealed from sight, some counterpoising weight equal to it; but it is still allowed to doubt, whether that weight be an aggregate of several distinct bodies, or one uniform united mass. And if the weight requisite very much exceeds any thing which we have ever seen conjoined in any single body, the former supposition becomes still more probable and natural. An intelligent being of such vast power and capacity as is necessary to produce the universe, or, to speak in the language of ancient philosophy, so prodigious an animal exceeds all analogy, and even comprehension.

But further, Cleanthes: men are mortal, and renew their species by generation; and this is common to all living creatures. The two great sexes of male and female, says Milton, animate the world. Why must this circumstance, so universal, so essential, be excluded from those numerous and limited deities? Behold, then, the theogony of ancient times brought back upon us.

And why not become a perfect Anthropomorphite? Why not assert the deity or deities to be corporeal, and to have eyes, a nose, mouth, ears, etc.? Epicurus maintained, that no man had ever seen reason but in a human figure; therefore the gods must have a human figure. And this argument, which is deservedly so much ridiculed by Cicero, becomes, according to you, solid and philosophical.

In a word, Cleanthes, a man who follows your hypothesis is able perhaps to assert, or conjecture, that the universe, sometime, arose from something like design: but beyond that position he cannot ascertain one single circumstance; and is left afterwards to fix every point of his theology by the utmost license of fancy and hypothesis. This world, for aught he knows, is very faulty and imperfect, compared to a superior standard; and was only the first rude essay of some infant deity, who afterwards abandoned it, ashamed of his lame performance: it is the work only of some dependent, inferior deity; and is the object of derision to his superiors: it is the production of old age and dotage in some superannuated deity; and ever since his death, has run on at adventures, from the first impulse and active force which it received from him. You justly give signs of horror, Demea, at these strange suppositions; but these, and a thousand more of the same kind, are Cleanthes's suppositions, not mine. From the moment the attributes of the Deity are supposed finite, all these have place. And I cannot, for my part, think that so wild and unsettled a system of theology is, in any respect, preferable to none at all.

These suppositions I absolutely disown, cried Cleanthes: they strike me, however, with no horror, especially when proposed in that rambling way in which they drop from you. On the contrary, they give me pleasure, when I see, that, by the utmost indulgence of your imagination, you never get rid of the hypothesis of design in the universe, but are obliged at every turn to have recourse to it. To this concession I adhere steadily; and this I regard as a sufficient foundation for religion. . . .

What you ascribe to the fertility of my invention, replied Philo, is entirely owing to the nature of the subject. In subjects adapted to the narrow compass of

same appearance of art and contrivance which we observe at present. All the parts of each form must have a relation to each other, and to the whole; and the whole itself must have a relation to the other parts of the universe; to the element in which the form subsists; to the materials with which it repairs its waste and decay; and to every other form which is hostile or friendly. A defect in any of these particulars destroys the form; and the matter of which it is composed is again set loose, and is thrown into irregular motions and fermentations, till it unite itself to some other regular form. If no such form be prepared to receive it, and if there be a great quantity of this corrupted matter in the universe, the universe itself is entirely disordered; whether it be the feeble embryo of a world in its first beginnings that is thus destroyed, or the rotten carcase of one languishing in old age and infirmity. In either case, a chaos ensues; till finite, though innumerable revolutions produce at last some forms, whose parts and organs are so adjusted as to support the forms amidst a continued succession of matter.

Suppose (for we shall endeavor to vary the expression), that matter were thrown into any position, by a blind, unguided force; it is evident that this first position must, in all probability, be the most confused and most disorderly imaginable, without any resemblance to those works of human contrivance, which, along with a symmetry of parts, discover an adjustment of means to ends, and a tendency to self-preservation. If the actuating force cease after this operation, matter must remain for ever in disorder, and continue an immense chaos, without any proportion or activity. But suppose that the actuating force, whatever it be, still continues in matter, this first position will immediately give place to a second, which will likewise in all probability be as disorderly as the first, and so on through many successions of changes and revolutions. No particular order or position ever continues a moment unaltered. The original force, still remaining in activity, gives a perpetual restlessness to matter. Every possible situation is produced, and instantly destroyed. If a glimpse or dawn of order appears for a moment, it is instantly hurried away, and confounded, by that never-ceasing force which actuates every part of matter.

Thus the universe goes on for many ages in a continued succession of chaos and disorder. But is it not possible that it may settle at last, so as not to lose its motion and active force (for that we have supposed inherent in it), yet so as to preserve an uniformity of appearance, amidst the continual motion and fluctuation of its parts? This we find to be the case with the universe at present. Every individual is perpetually changing, and every part of every individual; and yet the whole remains, in appearance, the same. May we not hope for such a position, or rather be assured of it, from the eternal revolutions of unguided matter; and may not this account for all the appearing wisdom and contrivance which is in the universe? Let us contemplate the subject a little, and we shall find, that this adjustment, if attained by matter of a seeming stability in the forms, with a real and perpetual revolution or motion of parts, affords a plausible, if not a true solution of the difficulty.

It is in vain, therefore, to insist upon the uses of the parts in animals or vegetables, and their curious adjustment to each other. I would fain know, how an animal could subsist, unless its parts were so adjusted? Do we not find, that it immediately perishes whenever this adjustment ceases, and that its matter corrupting tries some new form? It happens indeed, that the parts of the world are so well adjusted, that some regular form immediately lays claim to this corrupted matter: and if it were not so, could the world subsist? Must it not dissolve as well as the animal, and pass through new positions and situations, till in great, but finite succession, it falls at last into the present or some such order?

It is well, replied Cleanthes, you told us, that this hypothesis was suggested on a sudden, in the course of the argument. Had you had leisure to examine it, you would soon have perceived the insuperable objections to which it is exposed. No form, you say, can subsist, unless it possess those powers and organs requisite for its subsistence: some new order or economy must be tried, and so on, without intermission; till at last some order, which can support and maintain itself, is fallen upon. But according to this hypothesis, whence arise the many conveniences and advantages which men and all animals possess? Two eyes, two ears, are not absolutely necessary for the subsistence of the species. Human race might have been propagated and preserved, without horses, dogs, cows, sheep, and those innumerable fruits and products which serve to our satisfaction and enjoyment. If no camels had been created for the use of man in the sandy deserts of Africa and Arabia, would the world have been dissolved? If no loadstone had been framed to give that wonderful and useful direction to the needle, would human society and the human kind have been immediately extinguished? Though the maxims of Nature be in general very frugal, yet instances of this kind are far from being rare; and any one of them is a sufficient proof of design, and of a benevolent design, which gave rise to the order and arrangement of the universe.

At least, you may safely infer, said Philo, that the foregoing hypothesis is so far incomplete and imperfect, which I shall not scruple to allow. But can we ever reasonably expect greater success in any attempts of this nature? Or can we ever hope to erect a system of cosmogony, that will be liable to no exceptions, and will contain no circumstance repugnant to our limited and imperfect experience of the analogy of Nature? Your theory itself cannot surely pretend to any such advantage, even though you have run into *Anthropomorphism,* the better to preserve a conformity to common experience. Let us once more put into trial. In all instances which we have ever seen, ideas are copied from real objects, and are ectypal, not archetypal, to express myself in learned terms: you reverse this order, and give thought the precedence. In all instances which we have ever seen, thought has no influence upon matter, except where that matter is so conjoined with it as to have an equal reciprocal influence upon it. No animal can move immediately any thing but the members of its own body; and indeed, the equality of action and reaction seems to be an universal law of nature: but your theory implies a contradiction to this experience. These instances, with many more, which it were easy to collect, (particularly the supposition of a mind or system of thought that is eternal, or, in other words, an animal ingenerable and immortal); these instances, I say, may teach all of us sobriety in condemning each other, and let us see, that as no system of this kind ought ever to be received from a slight analogy, so neither ought any to be rejected on account of a small incongruity. For that is an inconvenience from which we can justly pronounce no one to be exempted.

All religious systems, it is confessed, are subject to great and insuperable difficulties. Each disputant triumphs in his turn; while he carries on an offensive war, and exposes the absurdities, barbarities, and pernicious tenets of his antagonist. But all of them, on the whole, prepare a complete triumph for the *Sceptic;* who tells them, that no system ought ever to be embraced with regard to such subjects: for this plain reason, that no absurdity ought ever to be assented to with regard to any subject. A total suspense of judgment is here our only reasonable resource. And if every attack, as is commonly observed, and no defence, among Theologians, is successful; how complete must be *his* victory, who remains always, with all mankind, on the offensive, and has himself no fixed station or abiding city, which he is ever, on any occasion, obliged to defend?

2. Immanuel Kant

[Kant, like Hume, has greater sympathy for the teleological "proof" than for any of the other forms of the
argument; but, again like Hume, he finds it inadequate. As the argument stands, it demonstrates only
that fitness and harmony exist in things according to
general laws, that is, the world is architectonic. But
this is not in itself adequate to prove that the world
is the result of a divine creator, an all-sufficient Being.
In order to demonstrate an all-sufficient Being, it is
necessary to have recourse to a transcendental "proof"
—the very problem that the principle of design intends
to avoid. Conceptions of absolute totality are, says
Kant, impossible when one is following a purely empirical path.]

Of the Impossibility of the Physico-Theological Proof*

If, then, neither the concept of things in general
[*ontological proof*], nor the experience of any *existence
in general* [*cosmological proof*] can satisfy our demands, there still remains one way open, namely, to
try whether any *definite experience*, and consequently
that of things in the world as it is, their constitution
and disposition, may not supply a proof which could

* From *Critique of Pure Reason*, translated by F. Max
Müller (New York, 1896).

give us the certain conviction of the existence of a Supreme Being. Such a proof we should call *physico-theological*. If that, however, should prove impossible too, then it is clear that no satisfactory proof whatever, from merely speculative reason, is possible, in support of the existence of a Being, corresponding to our transcendental idea.

After what has been said already, it will be easily understood that we may expect an easy and complete answer to this question. For how could there ever be an experience that should be adequate to an idea? It is the very nature of an idea that no experience can ever be adequate to it. The transcendental idea of a necessary and all sufficient original Being is so overwhelming, so high above everything empirical, which is always conditioned, that we can never find in experience enough material to fill such a concept, but can only grope about among things conditioned, looking in vain for the unconditioned, of which no rule of any empirical synthesis can ever give us an example, or even show the way towards it.

If the highest Being should stand itself in that chain of conditions, it would be a link in the series, and would, exactly like the lower links, above which it is placed, require further investigation with regard to its own still higher cause. If, on the contrary, we mean to separate it from that chain, and, as a purely intelligible Being, not comprehend it in the series of natural causes, what bridge is then open for reason to reach it, considering that all rules determining the transition from effect to cause, nay, all synthesis and extension of our knowledge in general, refer to nothing but possible experience, and therefore to the objects of the world of sense only, and are valid nowhere else?

This present world presents to us so immeasurable

a stage of variety, order, fitness, and beauty, whether we follow it up in the infinity of space or in its un-limited division, that even with the little knowledge which our poor understanding has been able to gather, all language, with regard to so many and inconceivable wonders, loses its vigour, all numbers their power of measuring, and all our thoughts their necessary de-termination; so that our judgment of the whole is lost in a speechless, but all the more eloquent astonish-ment. Everywhere we see a chain of causes and effects, of means and ends, of order in birth and death, and as nothing has entered by itself into the state in which we find it, all points to another thing as its cause. As that cause necessitates the same further inquiry, the whole universe would thus be lost in the abyss of nothing, unless we admitted something which, existing by itself, original and independent, outside the chain of infinite contingencies, should support it, and, as the cause of its origin, secure to it at the same time its permanence. Looking at all the things in the world, what greatness shall we attribute to that highest cause? We do not know the whole contents of the world, still less can we measure its magnitude by a comparison with all that is possible. But, as with re-gard to causality, we cannot do without a last and highest Being, why should we not fix the degree of its perfection *beyond everything else that is possible?* This we can easily do, though only in the faint out-line of an abstract concept, if we represent to our-selves all possible perfections united in it as in one substance. Such a concept would agree with the de-mand of our reason, which requires parsimony in the number of principles; it would have no contradictions in itself, would be favourable to the extension of the employment of reason in the midst of experience, by guiding it towards order and system, and lastly, would never be decidedly opposed to any experience.

This proof will always deserve to be treated with respect. It is the oldest, the clearest, and most in conformity with human reason. It gives life to the study of nature, deriving its own existence from it, and thus constantly acquiring new vigour.

It reveals aims and intention, where our own observation would not by itself have discovered them, and enlarges our knowledge of nature by leading us towards that peculiar unity the principle of which exists outside nature. This knowledge reacts again on its cause, namely the transcendental idea, and thus increases the belief in a supreme author to an irresistible conviction.

It would therefore be not only extremely sad, but utterly vain to attempt to diminish the authority of that proof. Reason, constantly strengthened by the powerful arguments that come to hand by themselves, though they are no doubt empirical only, cannot be discouraged by any doubts of subtle and abstract speculation. Roused from every inquisitive indecision, as from a dream, by one glance at the wonders of nature and the majesty of the cosmos, reason soars from height to height till it reaches the highest, from the conditioned to conditions, till it reaches the supreme and unconditioned Author of all.

But although we have nothing to say against the reasonableness and utility of this line of argument, but wish, on the contrary, to commend and encourage it, we cannot approve of the claims which this proof advances to apodictic certainty, and to an approval on its own merits, requiring no favour, and no help from any other quarter. It cannot injure the good cause, if the dogmatical language of the overweening sophist is toned down to the moderate and modest statements of a faith which does not require unconditioned submission, yet is sufficient to give rest and comfort. I therefore maintain that the physico-theological proof can never establish by itself alone the existence of a Supreme Being, but must always leave it to the ontological proof (to which it serves only as an introduction), to supply its deficiency; so that, after all, it is the ontological proof which contains the *only possible argument* (supposing always that any speculative proof is possible), and human reason can never do without it.

The principal points of the physico-theological proof are the following. 1st. There are everywhere in the world clear indications of an intentional arrangement carried out with great wisdom, and forming a whole indescribably varied in its contents and infinite in extent.

2ndly. The fitness of this arrangement is entirely foreign to the things existing in the world, and belongs to them contingently only; that is, the nature of different things could never spontaneously, by the combination of so many means, co-operate towards definite aims, if these means had not been selected and arranged on purpose by a rational disposing principle, according to certain fundamental ideas.

3rdly. There exists, therefore, a sublime and wise cause (or many), which must be the cause of the world, not only as a blind and all-powerful nature, by means of unconscious *fecundity,* but as an intelligence, by *freedom.*

4thly. The unity of that cause may be inferred with certainty from the unity of the reciprocal relation of the parts of the world, as portions of a skilful edifice, so far as our experience reaches, and beyond it, with plausibility, according to the principles of analogy.

Without wishing to argue, for the sake of argument only, with natural reason, as to its conclusion in inferring from the analogy of certain products of nature with the works of human art, in which man does violence to nature, and forces it not to follow its own aims, but to adapt itself to ours (that is, from the similarity of certain products of nature with houses, ships, and watches), in inferring from this, I say, that a similar causality, namely, understanding and will, must be at the bottom of nature, and in deriving the internal possibility of a freely acting nature (which, it may be, renders all human art and even human reason possible) from another though superhuman art—a kind of reasoning, which probably could not stand the severest test of transcendental criticism; we are willing to admit, nevertheless, that if we have to name such a cause, we cannot do better than to follow the analogy of such products of human design, which are the only ones of which we know completely both cause and effect. There would be no excuse, if reason were to surrender a causality which it knows, and have recourse to obscure and indemonstrable principles of explanation, which it does not know.

According to this argument, the fitness and harmony existing in so many works of nature might prove the contingency of the form, but not of the matter, that is, the substance in the world, because, for the latter purpose, it would be necessary to prove in addition, that the things of the world were in themselves incapable of such order and harmony, according to general laws, unless there existed, even in their *substance*, the product of a supreme wisdom. For this purpose, very different arguments would be required from those derived from the analogy of human art. The utmost, therefore, that could be established by such a proof, would be an *architect of the world,* always very much hampered by the quality of the material with which he has to work, not a *creator,* to whose idea everything is subject. This would by no means suffice for the purposed aim of proving an all-sufficient original Being. If we wish to prove the contingency of matter itself, we must have recourse to a transcendental argument, and this is the very thing which was to be avoided.

The inference, therefore, really proceeds from the order and design that can everywhere be observed in the world, as an entirely contingent arrangement, to the existence of a cause, *proportionate to it.* The concept of that cause must therefore teach us something quite *definite* about it, and can therefore be no other concept but that of a Being which possesses all might, wisdom, &c., in one word, all perfection of an all-sufficient Being. The predicates of a *very great,* of an astounding, of an immeasurable might and virtue give us no definite concept, and never tell us really what the thing is by itself. They are only relative representations of the magnitude of an object, which the observer (of the world) compares with himself and his own power of comprehension, and which would be equally grand, whether we magnify the object, or reduce the observing subject to smaller proportions in reference to it. Where we are concerned with the magnitude (of the perfection) of a thing in general, there exists no definite concept, except that which comprehends all possible perfection, and only the all (*omnitudo*) of reality is thoroughly determined in the concept.

Now I hope that no one would dare to comprehend the relation of that part of the world which he has observed (in its extent as well as in its contents) to omnipotence, the relation of the order of the world to the highest wisdom, and the relation of the unity of the world to the absolute unity of its author, &c. Physico-theology, therefore, can never give a definite concept of the highest cause of the world, and is insufficient, therefore, as a principle of theology, which is itself to form the basis of religion.

The step leading to absolute totality is entirely impossible on the empirical road. Nevertheless, that step is taken in the physico-theological proof. How then has this broad abyss been bridged over?

The fact is that, after having reached the stage of admiration of the greatness, the wisdom, the power, &c. of the author of the world, and seeing no further advance possible, one suddenly leaves the argument carried on by empirical proofs, and lays hold of that contingency which, from the very first, was inferred from the order and design of the world. The next step from that contingency leads, by means of transcendental concepts only, to the existence of something absolutely necessary, and another step from the absolute necessity of the first cause to its completely determined or determining concept, namely, that of an all-embracing reality. Thus we see that the physico-theological proof, baffled in its own undertaking, takes suddenly refuge in the cosmological proof, and as this is only the ontological proof in disguise, it really carries out its original intention by means of pure reason only; though it so strongly disclaimed in the beginning all connection with it, and professed to base everything on clear proofs from experience.

Those who adopt the physico-theological argument have no reason to be so very coy towards the transcendental mode of argument, and with the conceit of enlightened observers of nature to look down upon them as the cobwebs of dark speculators. If they would only examine themselves, they would find that, after they had advanced a good way on the soil of nature and experience, and found themselves nevertheless as much removed as ever from the object revealed to their reason, they suddenly leave that soil, to enter into the realm of pure possibilities, where on the wings of ideas they hope to reach that which had withdrawn itself from all their empirical investigations. Imagining themselves to be on firm ground after that desperate leap, they now proceed to expand the definite concept which they have acquired, they do not know how, over the whole field of creation; and they explain the ideal, which was merely a product of pure reason, by experience, though in a very poor way, and totally beneath the dignity of the object, refusing all the while to admit that they have arrived at that knowledge or supposition by a very different road from that of experience.

Thus we have seen that the physico-theological proof rests on the cosmological, and the cosmological on the ontological proof of the existence of one original Being as the Supreme Being; and, as besides these three, there is no other path open to speculative reason, the ontological proof, based exclusively on pure concepts of reason, is the only possible one, always supposing that any proof of a proposition, so far transcending the empirical use of the understanding, is possible at all.

C. THE CONTEMPORARY REJOINDER

1. A. E. TAYLOR (1869–1945)

[A. E. Taylor, who was professor of moral philosophy at the University of Edinburgh, is perhaps most noted for his detailed studies on Plato. He has also made significant contributions in the philosophy of religion. In the following essay, Professor Taylor reviews the question of natural and teleological order. Nature is pervaded, he argues, by "prospective adaptations." To account for these adaptations is the central problem of teleology. Reflection reveals that the option lies between a theory of coincidence, which confirms Darwin's process of natural selection, and some form of theistic cosmology whereby intelligence controls and directs the domain of the physical. Taylor concludes that teleology is a viable position because intelligence is most reasonably regarded not as something produced by an inert physical source but as itself an active force in the universe—a force that works toward the realization of ends.]

Nature and Teleology*

When we turn to the facts about living organisms which are the subject-matter of the biological sciences, we find ourselves at once confronted with what, on

* From *Does God Exist?* (London, 1945), Chapter IV. Reprinted by permission of Macmillan & Co., Ltd., London, and The Macmillan Company of Canada, Ltd.

the face of it, looks to be a further type of order in nature, *teleological* order. The way in which a process shall take place appears to be determined not simply by reference to the earlier stages of natural process of which it is the continuation, but even more by reference to the later and still future results which are to come out of the present. (Hence the name *teleological* order, from the Greek *telos, end*, last phase.)

It is not that the processes taking place in living organisms appear in any way to violate the causal laws of physics. On the contrary, it seems that, so far as can be ascertained, the behaviour of the components of the living organism conforms throughout to these laws. Thus transformations of energy taking place within the organism, like similar transformations in the realm of the inorganic, appear to conform strictly to the principle of Conservation of Energy; there is an increase or decrease of energy of a specific kind only at the cost of a proportional decrease or increase somewhere of energy of another kind. But the important point is this. There are indefinitely numerous ways in which a natural process can be continued in strict conformity with the principle of Conservation, just as there is a great (though not an indefinite) variety of ways in which a move may be made at chess without violating any of the rules of the game. But the healthy organism in normal conditions continues the process by responding to the present situation with just that continuation which is valuable as preserving the individual organism or making for the continuance of the species, just as the good chess-player meets his opponent's move by making just that reply out of the many open to him which is best adapted to achieve a result which still lies in the future, the winning of the game. Examples of this thorough-going adaptation of the behaviour of the living organism to a state of things which is still future are so common and obvious that it may be enough to mention only one or two. "Wherever there is need for an extra supply of oxygen, as, for instance, during muscular exertion, the membrane assumes an active rôle, and pushes oxygen inwards without regard to the mechanical laws of diffusion."[1] Here it is a need which the individual organism will experience in the immediate future which appears to determine just which of many mechanically equally possible responses shall be adopted. Numerous insects "instinctively" deposit their eggs on a particular kind of leaf which will supply suitable nourishment for the coming generation of grubs, though the insects themselves will die before the eggs are hatched. The principles of physics would be equally respected if any other kind of leaf evoked the same expenditure of energy in egg-depositing, but in fact it is evoked only by the special kind of leaf which will form the appropriate nourishment of creatures whom the egg-depositing insect will never live to see. Hence the adaptation is to a remoter future and the advantage secured is to the benefit of the still unborn offspring, not of the egg-depositing insect. The life of organic nature is pervaded throughout by "prospective adaptations" of this kind, and the problem is how to account for this patent fact.

It is the same, of course, with the familiar everyday life of human beings. But here we know, or think we know, the explanation of the fact. So far as the mechanical laws involved in its working are concerned,

[1] J. S. Haldane quoted in Stout, *Mind and Matter* (Cambridge University Press, 1931), p. 107.

it is all one to my gramophone whether it plays Palestrina or plays ragtime. If it plays Palestrina, that is because *I* have selected the record, and I have selected that record *prospectively* because I, or someone else whom I am wishing to entertain, would rather have that form of entertainment. If we would rather have ragtime, I should have put on a different record, and the mechanism of the instrument would equally readily have responded. The reason why it actually gives a Palestrina response is that this was the one I looked for and wanted. The machine does not give me Palestrina because it is so built that it can only do that one thing, as Lewis Carroll's baker could only bake bride-cake. Similarly, when I find that the egg-laying of a particular moth only happens on the leaves of the white poplar, I may properly ask, is this because something or someone wants the eggs laid on the particular kind of leaf which will be suitable food for the future grubs, or because the creature's egg-laying machinery happens to be so built that it can only work in that way? Is it just a coincidence that it is also the one way by which the grubs will be ensured of nourishment?

Or we may take a different illustration which sets our point in fuller relief. Consider the behaviour of a cat watching a mouse-hole, or stalking a small bird. Here we have an elaborate and highly complicated series of movements of the animal's whole body connected by the way in which the whole succession is adapted to a particular future event, the capture of the prey. It is this event yet to come which gives the whole series its distinctive character. As far as the working of the machinery which I call the cat's body is concerned, there might as well have been any one of a hundred other series of movements and arrests of movement which would have been in equal conformity with all the laws of physics, only none of these would have been equally successful in leading up to the capture. What has determined the selection of this particular series as against all the other possibilities is that all through the cat's movements have been adapted to the movements of the mouse or the bird, and not only to those which the mouse or bird has already made, but to those which it will make next, exactly as a good chessplayer's moves are determined not only by the moves his opponent has made, but to those which he will yet have to make. Can we completely account for the prospective attention which guides the whole course of the animal's behaviour by reference to the physical laws which are exemplified by every event in nature, organic and inorganic alike? This is the question which it is, I think, safe to say that all the most eminent psychologists—and the question is one for an expert in psychology, not for a chemist or a physicist, or even a biologist as such—are agreed to answer with, NO.

The laws of physics and chemistry—let me repeat again—as they can be discovered alike in the processes of the inorganic and of the organic realm do not provide any complete account of the characteristic behaviour of living creatures. It is not that anyone suggests that the processes going on in the living organism fail to conform to the various laws of physics, that of the Conservation of Energy and the rest: for all we know, these laws may be exactly exemplified in all these processes. The point is that there is a great outstanding characteristic of vital processes which the completest statement of the laws of physics leaves unaccounted for. As Whitehead has said, the electrons within the living organism, no doubt, run as "blindly" as the electrons in a lump of inorganic matter, but they do not run in the same way.[2] There are countless ways in which they might run, all of them in accord with the known laws of physics, but the actual way in which they do tend to run is always one which is "prospectively" adapted to the preservation of the individual organism or the species to which it belongs. While the organism is in normal health the tendency is actually successful; even in disease it persists; the organism reacts against the disorder by efforts to "right itself," or if they fail, it dies. But so far as the laws of physics alone are concerned, processes of "prospective" *misadaptation* stand on the same footing with, and should be just as probable as, those of prospective adaptation. This is inevitably so, for the simple reason that in the very formulation of a law of physics it is always assumed that the course of events in the future, which while it is still future is, of course, inaccessible to our observation and measurement, is determined entirely by reference to what has already occurred, been observed and measured. To introduce any reference to the still unborn future as playing a part in determining the present would be to introduce reference to a "factor" which, in the nature of the case, has not been, and could not have been, subjected to measurement. And this would be fatal to the whole purpose of a physical enquiry, the discovery of formulae which will permit us to calculate the as yet unobserved from measurements already made. For the purpose of such an enquiry we both necessarily and

[2] *Science and the Modern World* (New York, 1926), pp. 112 ff.

legitimately ignore the possibility of the prospective adaptation of the present event to an "end" still in the future.[3]

Yet such prospective adaptation is the most palpable and obvious character of the processes of organic life, and it has to be accounted for somehow. To put the point quite crudely: For one way in which the electrons which make up the organism can "blindly run" so as to secure this prospective adaptation, there are thousands of alternative ways, all alike conforming to the known laws of physics, in which they might run so as not to secure it. Hence if the laws of physics were a complete account of the conditions determining the course of natural processes, it would be antecedently immensely improbable that organisms should come into existence, or that, if by any accident they arose, they should persist. But it is the actual fact that they have arisen and display a remarkable power of

[3] Since these lines were written, Professor Laird has published his *Theism and Cosmology* (London, 1940). In Chapter VII of this work Professor Laird criticizes unfavourably the sort of language used in the preceding sentences. It is not, he contends, the future which in any case determines the present; for the future, until it has become present, is nothing at all. What does determine the purposive action of human beings is their expectations, hopes, fears about the future, and these are not themselves future. But, after all, it still remains true that, as Professor Laird himself remarks, pre-adaptation does not always depend on anticipatory "ideas." *Perhaps* it never depends on them in any cases known to us except those of human beings and, possibly, the highest animals, and yet such pre-adaptation is universal in the plant as well as in the animal "world." Hence the force of the argument for the presence throughout animated nature of an agency unknown to the sciences of the inorganic seems to me to remain unaffected. Professor Laird's insistence that the "future," so long as it is future, is just nothing at all, seems to me to show that he has not sufficiently emancipated himself from the Humean assumption (of which Hume himself saw the difficulty) that "all events are loose and separate."

persisting by adjusting themselves to their "environment". Unless we are to take refuge in a paradox like Tertullian's *certum est quia absurdum*, we can only draw the inference that the conditions taken into account in physics are not the only conditions which determine the course of processes within the living organism; there must be some further condition which removes what would otherwise be the indefinitely high improbability of the occurrence of that prospective adaptation which we see to be the fact in the realm of the organic.

Now there is just one known condition which, if we suppose it to be present, would remove this improbability, and that is the presence of *mind* as somehow determining the course of events. The one case in which the existence of mind as a fact is directly and immediately disclosed to us is our own, and nothing is clearer than that, in our own case, the distinctive character of mind is that, by its very nature, it is forward-reaching and shows its presence by the devising of adaptations to situations not yet present, but anticipated. It would, for example, be conclusive evidence that a man of advanced years had not sunk into a condition of complete dementia to show that he performs acts which are not merely responses to actual stimulus, and so adaptations to the present, but presuppose anticipation of situations which have not yet arisen and are preparatory adaptations to these anticipated situations. However enfeebled an old man's intellectual powers might be, no judge and jury would decide that his mind was completely "in abeyance," if it were proved that he had anticipated his own death and so expressed the wish to make a prospective disposition of his property. Similarly in a criminal case, if the defence set up were that the perpetrator of some deed were imbecile and incapable of understanding the "character of his action," the worth of the plea would depend on the court's judgement on the question whether the accused could anticipate what would come out of what he was doing. A man who places an obstacle on the road is "capable of understanding" the character of his action if he can *foresee* what may happen to a car driving along the road, "incapable" if he cannot. And speaking generally, we all in everyday life judge of a man's intelligence by the extent to which what he does and avoids doing is determined by purpose and intention, prospective adaptation to future situations before they arise. The more completely a man is emancipated from this determination by reference to the future, the more he lives simply in the present, the more "sub-human" and merely "animal" do we pronounce his way of living.

We have, indeed, already seen that there is a type of "scientific" man who seeks to deny the reality of purpose and intention as the outstanding characters of human conduct, and to reduce everything which ordinary men call intentional actions to complicated "conditioned reflexes" (that is, to account for everything that appears to be forward-looking action in human life by mere references to events of the present or the past). But—to pass over the express contradiction in the very statement of the theory already quoted from a prominent champion of it—we may safely say that its defenders themselves forget all about it as soon as they come out of their laboratories and studies and betake themselves to everyday social life. Like the rest of us, the deniers of the existence of the "soul" believe in practice that when they insure their lives, they do so to "make provision for those they may leave behind them"; that when they publish

essays deriding Christianity, they do it to help their
readers to escape from "superstition"; that when they
mark a ballot paper at a general election, they make
their cross "to do something for the return" of the
candidate they favour. And so long as every day of
their own lives proves that they have no real belief
in their own formulas, the rest of us may be excused if
we do not take their scientific heavy artillery to be
charged with anything more formidable than blank
powder.

The case, then, stands thus. Mind is, in its very
nature, forward-looking; in our own life, where the
evidence of its presence is direct and unmistakable, it
is impossible to escape recognizing that it guides and
shapes present action with a view to a future which
"does not yet appear." And, as we have seen already,
there is compelling reason for the view that mind is
not itself an effect called into being by the action of
physical agents, but *at least* a primitive underived
constituent of the real world, *at the very least* as real
as "matter" and "energy." Further, there is "prospective" adaptation to the future running through the
whole life of organized nature, though the lower down
we go in the scale of organisms the simpler such
adaptations are, and the less remote and more immediately impending the "future" to which the present
behaviour of the "organism" is seen to be adapted. A
man can adapt the whole scheme of his life to the
realization of a future that he will never live to see,
which perhaps generations of his descendants will not
live to see; he can build for "remote posterity". The
lower organisms cannot do this, yet there is in the
insect realm, for instance, a thorough-going adaptation
of the behaviour of one generation to the needs of a
fresh generation which will only come into being after

the death of the present. And again, to take another example, the "reactions" of the cat stalking its prey or the hunting dog have the same character of being prospective. They are "intelligent," though the intelligence they presuppose can hardly be only that of the cat or the dog, which are pretty clearly not conscious *why* they behave as they do. On the face of it, animal life seems to disclose intelligence everywhere adapting the present to the needs of the still unborn future, though, except in man, the directing intelligence does not appear to be embodied in the individual animal oganism. If we could suppose that the inorganic world has either existed all along or come into existence independently of intelligence, I do not see how we could avoid at least adding that with the advent of life we find intelligence somehow seizing upon and getting the direction of inanimate nature and its forces and turning them to its own account. This is, in fact, I conceive, the imaginative picture in the minds of many of those writers who allow themselves to put something which they call an *élan vital* or a *Life Force* into the place occupied by God in a Christian or a theistic cosmology. They hesitate to talk about a divine mind or a supreme intelligence, but they imagine life itself endowed with that prospective controlling and directing power with which we are familiar in mind, and picture it as somehow invading and capturing a foreign domain of the merely lifeless and physical.[4]

However attractive to the imagination, such a picture, I would urge, must be unsatisfactory to the intellect. We can easily understand how a human intelligence can utilize for its own purpose a piece of machinery which it has done nothing to construct.

[4] I am thinking less here of Bergson than of H. G. Wells and other "popular" writers. . . .

Every one of us has daily the occasion to use in this way numerous tools and instruments not of his own contrivance; with most of us it is the exception when we have ourselves *devised* any of the implements we use, and we accordingly plume ourselves on our ingenuity when, by way of an exception, we have constructed one of them for ourselves. But we must remember that the instrument which I did not myself fashion was fashioned by the contriving intelligence of someone else, and if it was not expressly designed to do precisely the work I do with it, it was expressly made to do some not wholly dissimilar piece of work.

Hence there is no really adequate analogy between my employment for some definite purpose of a tool which I did not myself make and the supposed capture of the wholly purposeless "machinery" of the inorganic world by a "life force." The appearance and persistence of living species, and still more the succession of increasingly purposeful and intelligent species, would be impossible without a preparatory adaptation of the "environment" to support and sustain the ascending series. With a different chemical constitution of the solar system, for example, the appearance of living organisms on our planet might have been impossible; even given the actual chemical constitution, it is easy to think of possible conditions of things which would have prevented our planet from being the habitat of creatures capable of attaining to science, or even to any experience or habit of customary expectation. Either we must be content to take it as an unexplained and inexplicable miracle that our environment should be one which has made the appearance of increasingly intelligent and purposeful species of organisms and the development of scientific knowledge possible, or we must carry back the presence of controlling and directing intelligence beyond the appearance of living species and admit that it has been at work throughout the whole history of the formation of the environment which is their indispensable background. If there is "design" in nature at all, design must be woven into the whole fabric of nature. If it is not so, the adaptation of the physical world to be the scene of the "emergence" of so much teeming purposeful life will be only a coincidence, and a coincidence of the kind which is infinitely improbable. Hence, as it seems to me (and I know that better philosophers than myself are of the same opinion), the vast expansion of our knowledge of the natural world in the last century or century and a half, so far from weakening the traditional "argument from design," has made it much stronger than it could have appeared in the days of Hume and Voltaire and Kant.[5]

Let us consider for a moment the general character of the counter-argument which might be produced in favour of what I have called the theory of coincidence. And to avoid underrating its strength, let us take the supposition which is most favourable to it,[6] that of

[5] It is just here that I own to finding difficulty in following the so-often inspiring thought of M. Bergson. It may be my own fault, but I have never been able to gather from his volumes an intelligible answer to the question where the *élan vital* gets the "dead matter" which it turns to its own purposes. Even in the *Deux Sources* it is not quite clear to me whether the God of whom the author speaks is really, in the full sense, Creator of all things visible and invisible, or only the Manichaean "Lord of the Kingdom of Light," engaged in a successful but never-ending war with a rival Prince of Darkness. He should be the former, to justify the writer's claims for him, but is he?

[6] I trust it will be understood that I am stating the argument for what may be called a rigidly "Darwinian" view, not because I believe it to be really tenable, but simply, as I say, in order that the case for what I call the "theory of coincidence" may not go by default. Personally, I am satisfied by the kind of

the correctness of a rigidly "Darwinian" doctrine of
the "origin of species," as though it were unquestion-
able, though, in point of fact, Darwin was not himself
a thorough-going "Darwinian," and, so far as a layman
can gather, the biologists of the present day are still
less so. That is, we will assume for the purpose of discussion that "natural selection" is a complete account
of the "origin of species." We are to think of organisms as perpetuating themselves by the repeated re-
production of the same pattern, subject only to minute
individual variations due to conditions too intricate
and complex for specification. These variations we are
to think of as taking place in all sorts of directions,
some of them being favourable to the organism's
chance of maintaining itself in being and reproducing
its life, some unfavourable, some neutral, and the
"laws of nature" are to be impartial as between these
three types of variation. But variations in any of these
directions, once introduced, are to perpetuate themselves, so that there is the possibility that in the course
of a great number of generations there may be an accumulation of many minute variations in the direction
of better adaptation to the environment sufficient to
constitute a recognizably distinct species. So much being assumed, we shall then reason thus.

Every individual variation which happens to be in
the direction of better adaptation to its environment,

criticism urged for example by Bergson in *L'Évolution Créatrice* that the conception of the origination of a new species by
the accumulation of "minute" differences is an illusion, though
a very natural illusion and one which it takes a metaphysician
to detect. I may again be told that it is unnecessary to discuss
the defects of such an "ultra-Darwinism," since no biologist
now really defends it. Yes, but the question is whether some
such position is not an indispensable part of a non-theistic metaphysics.

will, of course, have an improved, if only a minutely improved, chance of keeping itself alive and leaving behind it descendants which inherit its advantages. An accumulation of such favourable variations sufficient to constitute a new species will thus have a very great advantage in the competition for survival, with the result that less well-adapted competitors will, in the end, fail to maintain themselves in being, and will vanish from the world. In the end, then, we shall be left with a number of distinct surviving species which happen to be specially well fitted to their particular environment. It will look as though this adaptation were the result of intelligent design, but the appearance will be delusive. What has really occurred is only that the slow pressure of a relatively stable environment has eliminated all types but those which happen to be specially well suited to itself. (The process was called by Darwin natural *selection*, but we must, of course, carefully remember that word *selection*, though convenient, is clogged with misleading associations. There has been no *selecting*, no picking out of any individuals or types to survive, but only the gradual dying-off of those least able to adjust themselves to their situation, and this process of dying-off requires no directing intelligence for its explanation; the habitat makes its inhabitants by the simple process of killing off anyone who does not "fit in." We may call this the "survival of the fittest," but if we do so we must be careful to remember that the "fittest" do not mean the most highly gifted, the most intelligent, the most virtuous, or those who, by whatever standard of valuation we please to assume, are in some way "better" than their neighbours and rivals, but simply those who "fit in" to the habitat in question. The fittest in some environments may be the most versatile, or in-telligent, or morally deserving, but in others they may equally well be the most hide-bound, the stupidest or the most knavish. "It is the fittest to survive who sur-vive" amounts in fact to little more than the tautology that in the long run those who have the best chances of hanging-on in a specified environment are those who do hang on.)[7]

It is obvious that when a theory of this kind is put forward as explaining away all appearance of "design" in nature some large assumptions are being made about the actual facts and that these assumptions might conceivably be called in question. Is it a fact that individual variations from type occur impartially in every direction, or does variation exhibit a prepon-derant trend in some definite direction (in which case we should have at least a *prima facie* suggestion of purposive determination by an end)? And again, if the first view is the true one, is it by slow accumulation of such "random" minute variations that new species originate, or do they, as has been held more recently by some, come into being by sudden and considerable large-scale "mutations"? These are questions of fact which must be settled before the "Darwinian" theory can be regarded as established, and the facts are of a kind on which it is for the biological expert and for no one else to pronounce. It would be presumptuous for a layman in biology to assert an opinion of his

---

[7] Of course the statement just given really ignores the crux of the whole doctrine. However slow and gradual we may hold the accumulation of modifications to be, during the period while it is going on, the new species is not there, and so has not been "originated"; when it is there, at the end of the process, it has come into being all at once, "at a stroke."

own about them.[8] But without going into any disputable questions of fact, we can see, even though we may not be biological experts at all, that the whole theory is strictly what it originally professed to be, a theory about the way in which new species of organisms come into being. It is not a theory of the *origin* of organisms or of life; it takes organisms as known to be already in existence and professes only to explain how they are modified by the action of their environment upon them. It presupposes as already existing the antithesis between the living organism and the environment upon which and against which it maintains, or fails to maintain, itself. And, as we have already con-

---

[8] But we may be permitted to recall the dilemma insisted upon by Bergson in the first chapter of *L'Évolution Créatrice*, and illustrated by reference to the "evolution" of such an organ as the eye of vertebrates. Somehow the vertebrate eye has been "evolved" from the primitive pigmentary spot or speck, and it is assumed that the explanation of the development is that the individuals with the more highly developed organ of vision have consequently had the better chance of survival and leaving offspring. But any improvement in the eye which secures its possessor such an advantage is, in fact, a *complex* of countless co-ordinated changes of different kinds in a multitude of elements (retina, crystalline, cornea, etc.). The occurrence of one of these changes *without the rest* would, in fact, impair the vision of the creature and diminish its prospects of survival. To suppose that the whole complex of co-ordinated changes occur once for all by a sudden "mutation" is to suppose an immensely improbable "accident"; if, to avoid the improbability, we think of each change in the strict Darwinian fashion, as arising separately by a minute variation, it follows that during most of the period over which the process is going on there has been *no* advantage derived from the variations, and no reason, therefore, why they should have been preserved by "natural selection." The reasoning seems to me to be fatal to *any* theory of the origination of species in the course of "unguided" evolution. I would also refer the reader to the masterly examination of evolutionary philosophy in the late Professor James Ward's *Naturalism and Agnosticism* (London, 1915), Vol. I, pp. 185–272.

tended, purposiveness, determination of the present by reference to an end which is still in the future, is there wherever there is a living organism. The strictest "neo-Darwinism" thus offers us no explanation of the appearance of "prospective contrivance" in nature; on the contrary, it consciously or unconsciously assumes its reality, and therefore leaves our preceding argument unaffected. The suggestion so powerfully borne in upon the unsophisticated mind by a general survey of nature, that the rise and persistence of living organisms implies intelligent pre-adaptation of the lifeless background to be an "environment" for them is at least not weakened, it may be is strengthened, by increasing knowledge of the details of the adaptation. . . .

It would seem to follow that, as I have said already, human intelligence cannot coherently be explained as the final result of a mere long-continued slow process of the elimination of the "unfit." What such a process by itself should logically lead to would be a vast multiplicity of definite adjustments to definite situations, each being in fact conducive to some future result beneficial to the individual, or its species, or both. There is no reason in the nature of the case why these adjustments should be accompanied in man with foresight of the benefit to which they conduce, any more than in the insect which deposits its eggs only on the kind of leaf which will nourish grubs that the egg-layer will never live to see. And there is still less reason why the supposed process should lead to the kindling of an intelligence which is not content to adapt its behaviour to the situations furnished by the environment as they arise, but sets itself to transform the environment into conformity to its own demands. Given foreseeing intelligence as already existing and active in the world, we can understand that it might avail itself, for its own wider ends, of adaptation produced by the mere "survival of the fittest," and we can see that intelligence armed with these resources would enable its possessor to survive very effectively indeed. What is, to me at any rate, incredible that intelligence itself could be *produced* in the way supposed. Consideration of the way in which intelligence works in man thus seems to me to confirm the conclusion we have already reached on wider grounds, that there is no reason to think that intelligence has ever been "produced" at all, and every reason to think that it has not. And once more, if intelligence has always been active in the world, then we may assume that it has been active in the way which is characteristic and distinctive of intelligence, as working towards the realization of purpose. Thus the thought which is at the basis of the familiar "argument from design" will be thoroughly justified, and we shall see that Kant was right when he said in his *Critique of Pure Reason*, just before proceeding to a devastating attack upon the misuse of the argument in popular theology, that it "deserves never to be spoken of without reverence," and that it would be "utterly in vain to attempt to lessen its prestige."

What has told against this "prestige" in the judgement of more hasty thinkers than Kant has, in fact, been confusion between the substance of the "argument" and certain unjustifiable assumptions which are really unessential to it but have often been conjoined with it by well-meaning but inconsiderate divines and philosophers in a hurry to make out the case for Theism. It has too often been assumed that if the course of events is really directed by a purposive intelligence, the purpose of that intelligence must lie in some single result to be attained at the end of the world's history and to which all that precedes is a mere "means," as the scaffolding is a mere means to the erection of a house. There must be some one "far-off divine event" to which "the whole creation moves." To make this assumption is to take it for granted that the one typical example of the working of intelligence is to be seen in the crafts and industries, where it is true that the whole elaborate process of construction has no worth or interest except as a means to the existence of the manufactured article. But the making of houses, or ships, or (to take Paley's famous example) watches is not the only, and I think we may say not the supreme, example of constructive intelligence. Intelligence is also shown, and as most of us would perhaps say, is more triumphantly shown, in the fashioning of a great poem or drama or symphony. But it would be ridiculous to say that in *Paradise Lost* or *Hamlet* or the *Eroica* symphony the whole work is a mere means to the final paragraph or scene or chord. All three are intensely purposive, but the purpose of Milton or Shakespeare or Beethoven is to make a work which shall be throughout a thing of high beauty, with the inherent worth which belongs to a beautiful thing. The beauty is not concentrated in the closing lines or notes, it is, except where the artist's performance falls short of his intentions, diffused over the whole. If we are to talk about "means" at all, the last book of the poem, the last scene of the tragedy, the last movement of the symphony are as much "means" to all that has preceded them, as it is to them. For its own full effect the close must be led up to by *this* beginning and *this* middle and no other; equally *this* beginning and middle, as we say, "call for" this ending; it also is a "means" to them, since they would not be beautiful as they are if they had led up to a different close. A work of art is defective if the beauties of any of its parts are only "incidental," irrelevant to their places as parts in this particular whole. It is true that all deep and vital religion does hold that the world's history leads up to a final result which lies outside and beyond that history, but it is not essential to the "argument from design" that this should be so. Even if the meaning and value of that history could be shown to lie entirely in itself, this would leave the general argument for the presence of purpose throughout that history unaffected.

Again, it is not implied in the argument that we human beings must have the key to all the designs of the intelligence controlling the course of the world's history, and it would be strange if we had. Each of us knows well enough that he is often in the dark as to the precise purposes which direct the conduct of his neighbours; he may be quite sure that they are acting with a purpose, though quite unable to say what that purpose is. And I think any one of us who is himself neither a Milton nor a Shakespeare nor a Beethoven must feel that it would be intolerable presumption in him to profess that he knows what is *the* purpose dominating their great works. In a general way, we can no doubt say that the purpose of a Milton in giving the best years of his life to composing *Paradise Lost* is to make a thing of high beauty. But things of high beauty are many and different, and we may be sure that Milton had some more definite purpose than this in making just this poem and no other; what that more definite purpose was, we shall, if we are modest men, admit that we can only know so far as the poet himself has been pleased to tell us; the rest is his secret. It would be still more presumptuous to assume that if there is a divine purpose in the history of the universe we can say, apart from any appeal to something which we take to be an actual "revelation" emanating from God Himself,[9] precisely what that purpose is. At most we can say that such a purpose, whatever it is, must be a wise and a good one. We have no right to assume further that it could only be the widest diffusion of the maximum pleasure over the creation. God may have some purpose with His creatures different from that of giving them all as much enjoyment as possible; indeed, on reflection, we might see reason to hold that to "make everyone jolly" at all costs would be a purpose worthy neither of divine wisdom nor of divine goodness. Hence it is no proof of the absence of intellect and moral purpose from the universe at large to dwell, as has so often been done, on the presence of so much suffering which we cannot see to fulfil any good purpose, or on the frequent prosperity of the vicious and ill-fortune of the virtuous. These familiar facts are at most no more than "difficulties"; they make it hard for us to recognize wise and beneficent purpose in the course of events. But if our general argument for the presence and operation of intelligence throughout the universe is sound, and if we can further give equally sound reasons for holding that the world-directing intelligence must be morally good as well as intelligent, these difficulties are no solid ground for

[9] The qualifying clause is important. It is not presumption in me to say that part of Milton's purpose was to "assert eternal Providence," for Milton himself has told me so. It is not presumptuous to draw certain inferences about the purpose of the *Eroica* from Beethoven's own original dedication of the work to Bonaparte and his cancellation of that dedication when Bonaparte turned into the *Emperor* Napoleon. So if I say that God has certain purposes for man, I am not falling into presumption, if there is reason to hold that my knowledge is due to a disclosure from God Himself.

since this implies not only a craving and an idea of what would satisfy it, but in addition knowledge, or at least beliefs, as to what actions would or might bring into existence that which would satisfy the craving. It may be objected that we do not understand *how* an obscure craving to see can generate an eye or at least the bodily variations which gradually culminate in an eye. But we do not understand in the least better *how* the craving of a designer external to man, that man shall have an eye, can generate without hands or tools that eye in man. Hence, if we suppose a craving to be somehow capable of doing the trick, it is more economical to locate it in the animal himself, who at least is known to exist, than in an external designer, whose existence is purely supposititious and not in the least more explanatory.

The considerations appealed to by the Argument from Design thus do not, when their implications are developed logically, contribute anything that would support the hypothesis of an omniscient, omnipotent, and perfectly good designer. Rather, they militate against it. The only sort of God compatible with, though not evidenced by, the observable facts would be, as John Stuart Mill perceived, a God possibly great but nevertheless limited in power, or knowledge, or goodness, or in any two or all three of these respects.

3. C. D. BROAD (1887–)

[Charles Dunbar Broad's analytical work in ethics, theory of knowledge, and the philosophy of religion has spanned half a century, and his contributions are of considerable importance. He is well known for concise distinctions; and the section that follows, in which he sets forth the features of various teleological systems, is a representative example. It is to be noted that the final portion of the essay does not represent Professor Broad's own position; rather, he is concerned only to demonstrate that this interpretation is the logical result of biological mechanism.]

Teleology, Mechanism, and Design*

I have so far discussed Mechanism and its alternatives in a perfectly general way; and have said nothing in detail concerning those peculiar facts about living organisms which make it plausible to distinguish a "Vital Order" with "ultimate characteristics" of its own. Now the peculiarities of living organisms are often summed up in the phrase that organisms are "Teleological Systems." And there is thought to be some special connexion between Teleology and Design, and some special opposition between Teleology and Mech-

* From *The Mind and Its Place in Nature* (London, 1925). Reprinted by permission of Routledge & Kegan Paul, Ltd. and Humanities Press, Inc.

anism. I shall end this chapter by trying to clear up these points.

Teleology is an observable characteristic which certainly belongs to some things in the world. Design is a particular cause which certainly produces teleology in some cases. I want to begin by defining "teleology" in such a way that there shall be no doubt of its existence and that the admission of this fact shall not presuppose the acceptance of any special theory. Suppose that a system is composed of such parts arranged in such ways as might have been expected *if* it had been constructed by an intelligent being to fulfil a certain purpose which he had in mind. And suppose that, when we investigate the system more carefully under the guidance of this hypothesis, we discover hitherto unnoticed parts or hitherto unnoticed relations between the parts, and that these are still found to accord with the hypothesis. Then I should call this system "teleological." It will be noticed that there are two clauses in the definition. The first is that our more or less superficial knowledge of the system suggests that it was designed for a special purpose which a rational mind might be likely to entertain. The second is that, if we use this hypothesis as a clue to more minute investigation, we continue to find that the system is constructed as if the hypothesis were true. I think that probably both factors are necessary. Of any system whatever we might suppose that it was designed to do what we actually find it doing. But in general we should not find that this gave us any clue to investigating its more minute structure or predicting its unobserved behaviour.

Now it seems to me perfectly certain that the world contains systems which are teleological, in this sense. The most obvious examples of such systems are machines, like watches, motor-cars, etc. In this case of course we start by knowing that they have in fact been designed by intelligent beings for a certain purpose, such as telling the time or conveying people quickly along roads. Knowing this we can explain, as we say, "what each part is for." Suppose now we were to meet with a certain machine for the first time and to know nothing about the purpose of its constructor. As we have met with plenty of other machines (though none exactly like this); as we know that all of these have been made by some human being for some purpose; and as we know of no machines which have arisen in any other way; we may legitimately infer that this one also was constructed by a human being for some purpose. By studying the action of the machine we may then be able to guess what the purpose probably was. We can then predict how it will probably be constructed in detail, and how it will probably work under various circumstances. And, if our predictions are found to be true, it is likely that we have hit on the true purpose of the machine. I will call the kind of teleology which is shown by watches, motor-cars, and other artificial machines, "external teleology." By this I mean that the purpose for which such systems were constructed, and by which their minute structure can be anticipated, is not wholly or mainly to keep themselves going or to produce other machines like themselves. Their main function is to do something, such as telling the time, which is of interest not to themselves but to their makers or other men.

Now it seems to me equally clear that living organisms are teleological systems in the sense defined. The most superficial knowledge of organisms does make it look as if they were very complex systems designed to preserve themselves in face of varying and threatening external conditions and to reproduce their kind. And, on the whole, the more fully we investigate a living organism in detail the more fully does what we discover fit in with this hypothesis. One might mention, *e.g.*, the various small and apparently unimportant glands in the human body whose secretions are found to exercise a profound influence over its growth and well-being. Or again we might mention the production in the blood of antitoxins when the body is attacked by organisms likely to injure it. I will call this kind of teleology "internal teleology." Whatever be the right explanation of it, it is plainly a fact.

We have now to consider the relation between Teleology and Design. (i) The definition of "teleology" involves a hypothetical reference to design. The system is teleological provided it acts *as if* it were designed for a purpose. But it does not involve anything more than this. It remains a question of fact whether the system was actually the result of a design in someone's mind. (ii) So far as we know, the teleology of non-living machines is always due to design. They behave in the characteristic way in which they do behave simply because their parts are constructed and fitted together in certain special ways, and we have no reason to suppose that this special arrangement could arise spontaneously without the intervention of a mind which deliberately chose it. (iii) The real paradox about organisms is that they are teleological systems which seem nevertheless to arise without design. It is this last fact which we must now discuss.

Many organisms have minds connected with them. But we know that, if they were designed at all, the mind which designed them was certainly not the mind which animates them, unless this be extraordinarily different from what it appears to be both to itself and to others. The highest type of mind which we are acquainted with is that which animates a human body. If we designed our own organisms we are quite unaware of the fact. And the enterprise seems altogether beyond our powers. The most skilled physiologist does not know how to make a living body; but, if we say that his mind designed his own organism, we must suppose that it performed as an embryo a feat which it is totally incapable of performing in its developed state. We must say then that, if organisms are designed by minds, either (*a*) the designing mind is altogether different from and enormously wiser and more skilful than the animating mind; or (*b*) that the animating mind, as known to itself by introspection and to others by communication, is the merest fragment of the total animating mind, and that the part of it which does not appear to itself or to others is of superhuman wisdom and ingenuity. Of course it might be held that the designing mind, or the designing part of the animating mind, though extraordinarily clever at its own particular job, takes no interest in anything else; or that it works in a wholly different way from the minds which are known to us. But this will not help us. If the conception of design is to provide any explanation of the peculiarities of organisms we must mean by "design" something of the same nature as the only designs that we know anything about, viz., our own. Otherwise we are merely playing with words. Now we have designs only when we imagine a possible state of affairs, apply our knowledge of the properties and laws of matter to discover how it might be brought about, and then use our technical skill to shape the material and to arrange it in those ways which we have seen to be necessary for our purpose. If the minds which design organisms act in this way they must have a superhuman knowledge of the laws and properties of matter, superhuman mathematical ability to work out the consequences of various possible combinations, and superhuman technical skill; and all analogy makes it most unlikely that a mind which took no interest in anything but the one job of manufacturing organisms would have these powers. If, on the other hand, the minds which design organisms act in some quite different and to us unknown way, then we have no right to call them "minds" or to call their mode of operation "design." We are merely assuming a wholly mysterious cause for the teleology of organisms, and tricking ourselves into the belief that it is an explanation by using the familiar words "mind" and "design." I conclude then that, if organisms be the result of design in any intelligible sense, their designers may fairly be called "gods"; and either we are gods in disguise or there are superhuman beings who make organisms.

These considerations remove one positive argument in favour of the theory of entelechies. I am sure that many people who look with a friendly eye on entelechies do so because of the teleological nature of organisms. They think of entelechies as little minds which design organisms and direct and control their growth and reactions. But they modestly regard entelechies as very inferior minds or as the inferior parts of the minds which animate organisms. Now, if I am right, this modesty is wholly out of place. If the hypothesis of an entelechy is to explain anything, we must suppose that an entelechy is a very superior mind or the very superior part of the mind which animates an organism. The theory insinuates itself into our confidence by pretending that the entelechy is so lowly a mind as scarcely to deserve the name; but it can explain the facts only if it supposes the entelechy to be so exalted a mind as to deserve the name of a "god."

I pass now to the relations between Teleology and Design, on the one hand, and Biological Mechanism, on the other. It is evident that, up to a point, there is no opposition between teleology and mechanism. Nothing can be more thoroughly teleological than a watch or a motor-car; yet these are machines, and their characteristic behaviour is wholly deducible from the special arrangement of their parts and from the general laws which these parts would equally obey in isolation or in other and non-teleological complexes. We may say then that, so long as we take a material system as a going concern and do not raise questions about its origin, there is no reason whatever why its characteristic behaviour should not be at once teleological and capable of complete mechanistic explanation. Now the mechanistic biologist regards organisms as very complex machines; and indeed if we were not very familiar with artificial self-acting and self-regulating machinery it would never have entered our heads to suggest a mechanistic theory of vital behaviour. So long as he confines his attention to a developed organism there is nothing preposterous in this theory. It is only when we consider the *origin* of teleological systems that a legitimate doubt arises whether teleology and mechanistic explanation are *ultimately* consistent with each other.

(i) Every system which is *certainly known* to be at once teleological and mechanistic is an artificial machine; and, if we follow its history far enough backwards, we always come to one or more *organisms*, which are teleological but not *certainly* mechanistic systems. It is true that many machines are themselves made by machines; but sooner or later in this chain we come to human bodies which made these machines and were not themselves made by machinery. Thus, apart altogether from any question of minds and their designs, there is something dangerously like a vicious circle in professing to explain the teleology of organisms by analogy with artificial machines. For, the moment we begin to consider the *origin* of organisms in general or of any particular organism, we have to admit that *all* artificial machines were ultimately made by organisms whilst *no* organism is ever made by an artificial machine.

To this objection I think that the following answer might be made. It might be said: "Admittedly we must distinguish two kinds of machines, viz., natural and artificial. We can quite well admit the general principle that *all* machines are made by other machines. Natural machines (*i.e.* organisms) are always made by other natural machines; artificial machines may be made proximately by other artificial machines, but in the long run in the history of any artificial machine we come to a natural machine. We admit then that natural machines are *causally* prior to artificial machines; but this involves no logical circle. We first derive the general notion of machinery and of a mechanistic explanation of teleological behaviour from the specially simple and obvious case of artificial machines, at a time when we do not suspect that our bodies are themselves natural machines. Eventually we *apply* the notion thus derived to our bodies, and find that it fits them perfectly. There is no inconsistency between the facts (*a*) that the recognition of artificial machines is psychologically prior to the recognition of natural machines, and (*b*) that the existence of natural machines is causally prior to the existence of artificial machines." I think that this is a valid answer to the particular logical objection raised above. But it does not exhaust the difficulties of Biological Mechanism; and this brings us to our next point.

(ii) It is true, but it is not the whole truth, to say that in the history of every system which is positively known to be both teleological and mechanistic (*i.e.* of every artificial machine) we come at length to an organism. We also come to the mind which animates this organism; to a design in this mind; and to the deliberate arrangement of matter in view of an end. And this seems to be essential for the production of a teleological system out of non-teleological materials. On a mechanistic theory the teleological behaviour of a system must be due wholly to the initial configuration of its parts; and, if matter has only the properties which physicists and chemists ascribe to it, it has no tendency by itself to fall into those extraordinarily special arrangements which alone can give rise to teleological behaviour. Now, if the analogy of organisms to artificial machines is to be used at all, it must be used fairly; we must not ignore one essential part of the facts about the origin of artificial machines. Let us then apply the whole analogy to organisms. It is certain that, when one organism produces another by ordinary processes of generation, the mind of the first does not design and construct the second, as it would if it were producing an artificial machine like a watch or a type-writer. This in itself need cause no trouble to the Mechanist. When one artificial machine produces another the mind of the first does not design the second, for artificial machines have no minds. The Biological Mechanist will therefore simply say that the generation of one organism by another is analogous to the production of one artificial machine by another. But, as we have seen, the latter series eventually brings us back to a mind with designs. Hence, if the Biological Mechanist is to apply his analogy fairly, there are only two courses open to him. The first is to say that there always have been organisms, and that organisms have never arisen from inorganic matter. On this alternative he has a series of natural machines going back to infinity. In that case of course every artificial machine will also have an infinite ancestry of other machines, since the production of an artificial machine eventually brings one back to a natural machine. Such a theory would be self-consistent; though it would still leave the awkward difference that design enters into the history of *every* artificial machine and of *no* natural machine. It is of course an alternative that most mechanists would be very loath to take; for one of the advantages claimed for Biological Mechanism over Substantial Vitalism is that the former does and the latter does not render the development of living from non-living matter conceivable.

The other possible alternative is to admit that organisms arose in the remote past out of non-living matter. This means, on the mechanistic view, that natural machines arose from matter which was not arranged in the form of a machine. And this can be consistently held *only* if the Biological Mechanist will postulate at that point the intervention of a mind which deliberately designed and arranged non-living matter in the form of a natural machine. For, as we have seen, the only systems which we positively *know* to be machines have all arisen in this way; and, if matter has no properties except those which chemists and physicists assign to it, there is not the least reason to suppose that it can spontaneously fall into the extremely special configuration which is needed if the resulting system is to behave teleologically. Thus the proper complement to a completely mechanistic theory about organisms is some form of the doctrine of Deism; a result which accords very well with that simple piety which is so characteristic of Biological Mechanists.

But, even if we are willing to go thus far with the Biological Mechanist, we cannot allow him to leave the matter there. Every system which is positively known to be a machine has been ultimately made, not by a pure spirit, but by a mind which animates an organism which it did not design or construct. This mind formed a design; in consequence of this the organism which it animates has moved in various ways; and it is thus and thus only that the design has been realised in foreign matter. Once more, if we are to use the analogy of machines at all, we must use it fairly and not ignore these parts of it which, so far as we can see, are essential but which are not convenient. The Biological Mechanist, having been brought willingly or unwillingly to Deism, must now take a further step and ascribe to God an organism which God's mind animates. And by all analogy we must suppose that God did not design or construct his own organism; since, so far as our experience goes *no* mind designs or constructs the organism which it animates. Thus, in the end, we shall be brought to one organism at least, viz., God's, which presumably has not arisen out of non-living matter either spontaneously or by design. This seems to be the final result of seriously and fairly applying the analogy between organisms and machines, when we cease to confine our attention to the organism as a going concern and try to account also for the origin of organisms, as Biological Mechanism would wish to do.

PAR[T]

A CONCLUDING

POST[SCRIPT]

A. J. J. C. SMART (1920–   )

[J. J. C. Smart is professor of philosophy at the University of Adelaide, South Australia. The present essay is an excellent example of philosophical analysis applied to issues in natural theology. Professor Smart maintains that the traditional arguments are philosophically unwarranted, because they incorrectly assume that logically necessary propositions affirm the truth of existential propositions. Such an assumption is self-contradictory. Nevertheless, he acknowledges the desire of most individuals to go on asking these questions and admits that answers have always functioned as potent instruments for religious conviction and emotion. Professor Smart's analysis of the ontological argument is included, since it is an integral part of the entire discussion.]

The Existence of God*

This lecture is not to discuss whether God exists. It is to discuss reasons which philosophers have given for saying that God exists. That is, to discuss certain arguments.

First of all it may be as well to say what we may hope to get out of this. Of course, if we found that any of the traditional arguments for the existence of

* From the *Church Quarterly Review* (1955). Reprinted by permission of the author.

God were sound, we should get out of our one hour this Sunday afternoon something of inestimable value, such as one never got out of any hour's work in our lives before. For we should have got out of one hour's work the answer to that question about which, above all, we want to know the answer. (This is assuming for the moment that the question 'Does God exist?' is a proper question. The fact that a question is all right as far as the rules of ordinary grammar are concerned does not ensure that it has a sense. For example, 'Does virtue run faster than length?' is certainly all right as far as ordinary grammar is concerned, but it is obviously not a meaningful question. Again, 'How fast does time flow?' is all right as far as ordinary grammar is concerned, but it has no clear meaning. Now some philosophers would ask whether the question 'Does God exist?' is a proper question. The greatest danger to theism at the present moment does not come from people who deny the validity of the arguments for the existence of God, for many Christian theologians do not believe that the existence of God can be proved, and certainly nowhere in the Old or New Testaments do we find any evidence of people's religion having a metaphysical basis. The main danger to theism today comes from people who want to say that 'God exists' and 'God does not exist' are equally absurd. The concept of God, they would say, is a nonsensical one. Now I myself shall later give grounds for thinking that the question 'Does God exist?' is not, in the full sense, a proper question, but I shall also give grounds for believing that to admit this is not necessarily to endanger theology.)

However, let us assume for the moment that the question 'Does God exist?' is a proper question. We now ask: Can a study of the traditional proofs of the existence of God enable us to give an affirmative answer to this question? I contend that it can not. I shall point out what seem to me to be fallacies in the main traditional arguments for the existence of God. Does proving that the arguments are invalid prove that God does not exist? Not at all. For to say that an argument is invalid is by no means the same thing as to say that its conclusion is false. Still, if we do find that the arguments we consider are all fallacious, what do we *gain* out of our investigation? Well, one thing we gain is a juster (if more austere) view of what philosophical argument can do for us. But, more important, we get a deeper insight into the logical nature of certain concepts, in particular, of course, the concepts of deity and existence. Furthermore we shall get some hints as to whether philosophy can be of any service to theologians, and if it can be of service, some hints as to how it can be of service. I think that it can be, but I must warn you that many, indeed perhaps the majority, of philosophers today would not entirely agree with me here.

One very noteworthy feature which must strike anyone who first looks at the usual arguments for the existence of God is the extreme brevity of these arguments. They range from a few lines to a few pages. St. Thomas Aquinas presents five arguments in three pages! Would it not be rather extraordinary if such a great conclusion should be got so easily? Before going on to discuss any of the traditional arguments in detail I want to give general grounds for suspecting anyone who claims to settle a controversial question by means of a short snappy argument.

My reason for doubting whether a short snappy argument can ever settle any controversial question is as follows: *any argument can be reversed*. Let me explain this. A question of elementary logic is involved. Let us consider an argument from two premisses, *p*, *q*, to a conclusion *r*:

$$\frac{\begin{array}{c}p\\q\end{array}}{r}$$

If the argument is valid, that is, if *r* really does follow from *p* and *q*, the argument will lead to agreement about *r* provided that there already is agreement about *p* and *q*. For example, if we have the premisses

p All A, B and C grade cricketers are entitled to a free pass to the Adelaide Oval for Test matches, Sheffield Shield matches, etc. (quite uncontroversial, it can be got from the rules of the South Australian Cricket Association).

q John Wilkin is an A, B or C grade cricketer. (Quite uncontroversial, everyone knows it.)

we may conclude

r John Wilkin is entitled to a free pass to the Adelaide Oval for Test matches, Sheffield Shield matches, etc.

But we now consider this argument[1]:

p Nothing can come into existence except through the activity of some previously existing thing or being.

q The world had a beginning in time.

therefore

r The world came into existence through the activity of some previously existing thing or being.

---

[1] I owe this illustration, and the whole application to the idea of 'reversing the argument', to Prof. D. A. T. Gasking of Melbourne.

If this argument is valid (as it certainly is) then it is equally the case that

(not-r) The world did not come into existence through the activity of some previously existing thing or being

implies that either

(not-p) Something *can* come into existence otherwise than through the activity of a previously existing thing or being

or

(not-q) The world had no beginning in time.

That is, if $\dfrac{p}{\dfrac{q}{r}}$ is valid $\dfrac{\text{not-}r}{\dfrac{q}{\text{not-}p}}$ and $\dfrac{\text{not-}r}{\dfrac{p}{\text{not-}q}}$ must be equally valid.

Now it is possible that a person might think that we have *fewer* reasons for believing r than we have for believing (not-p) or (not-q). In which case the argument $\dfrac{p}{\dfrac{q}{r}}$ though perfectly valid will not convince him. For he will be inclined to argue in the opposite direction, that is, from the falsity of r to the falsity of either p or q.

This last example is perhaps itself a—not very good —argument for the existence of God, but I have given it purely as an example to show *one* of the things to look out for when criticizing more serious arguments. The other thing to look out for, of course, is whether the argument is *valid*. It is my belief that in the case of any metaphysical argument it will be found that if the premises are uncontroversial the argument is unfortunately not valid, and that if the argument is valid the premises will unfortunately be just as doubtful as the conclusion they are meant to support.

With these warnings in mind let us proceed to the discussion of the three most famous arguments for the existence of God. These are:

(1) The Ontological Argument.
(2) The Cosmological Argument.
(3) The Teleological Argument.

The first argument—the ontological argument—really has no premisses at all. It tries to show that there would be a contradiction in denying that God exists. It was first formulated by St. Anselm and was later used by Descartes. It is not a convincing argument to modern ears, and St. Thomas Aquinas gave essentially the right reasons for rejecting it. However, it is important to discuss it, as an understanding of what is wrong with it is necessary for evaluating the second argument, that is, the cosmological argument. This argument does have a premiss, but not at all a controversial one. It is that something exists. We should all, I think, agree to that. The teleological argument is less austere in manner than the other two. It tries to argue to the existence of God not purely *a priori* and not from the mere fact of *something* existing, but from the actual features we observe in nature, namely those which seem to be evidence of design or purpose.

We shall discuss these three arguments in order. I do not say that they are the only arguments which have been propounded for the existence of God, but they are, I think, the most important ones. For example, of St. Thomas Aquinas' celebrated 'Five Ways' the first three are variants of the cosmological argument, and the fifth is a form of the teleological argument.

The Ontological Argument. This as I remarked, contains no factual premiss. It is a *reductio-ad-absurdum* of the supposition that God does not exist. Now *reductio-ad-absurdum* proofs are to be suspected whenever there is doubt as to whether the statement to be proved is *significant*. For example, it is quite easy, as anyone who is familiar with the so-called Logical Paradoxes will know, to produce a not *obviously* nonsensical statement, such that both it *and* its denial imply a contradiction. So unless we are sure of the significance of a statement we cannot regard a *reductio-ad-absurdum* of its contradictory as proving its truth. This point of view is well known to those versed in the philosophy of mathematics; there is a well-known school of mathematicians, led by Brouwer, who refuse in certain circumstances to employ *reductio-ad-absurdum* proofs. However, I shall not press this criticism of the ontological argument, for this criticism is somewhat abstruse (though it has been foreshadowed by Catholic philosophers, who object to the ontological argument by saying that it does not first show that the concept of an infinitely perfect being is a *possible* one). We are at present assuming that 'Does God exist?' is a proper question, and if it is a proper question there is no objection so far to answering it by means of a *reductio-ad-absurdum* proof. We shall content ourselves with the more usual criticisms of the ontological argument.

The ontological argument was made famous by Descartes. It is to be found at the beginning of his Fifth Meditation. As I remarked earlier it was originally put forward by Anselm, though I am sorry to say that to read Descartes you would never suspect that fact! Descartes points out that in mathematics we can deduce various things purely *a priori*, 'as for example', he says, 'when I imagine a triangle, although there is not and perhaps never was in any place . . . one such figure, it remains true nevertheless that this figure possesses a certain determinate nature, form, or essence, which is . . . not framed by me, nor in any degree dependent on my thought; as appears from the circumstance, that diverse properties of the triangle may be demonstrated, for example that its three angles are equal to two right, that its greatest side is subtended by its greatest angle, and the like'. Descartes now goes on to suggest that just as having the sum of its angles equal to two right angles is involved in the idea of a triangle, so *existence* is involved in the very idea of an infinitely perfect being, and that it would therefore be as much of a contradiction to assert that an infinitely perfect being does not exist as it is to assert that the three angles of a triangle do not add up to two right angles or that two of its sides are not together greater than the third side. We may then, says Descartes, assert that an infinitely perfect being *necessarily* exists, just as we may say that two sides of a triangle are together *necessarily* greater than the third side.

This argument is highly fallacious. To say that a so-and-so exists is not in the least like saying that a so-and-so has such-and-such a property. It is not to amplify a concept but to say that a concept applies to something, and whether or not a concept applies to something can not be seen from an examination of the concept itself. Existence is not a property. 'Growling' is a property of tigers, and to say that 'tame tigers growl' is to say something about tame tigers, but to say 'tame tigers exist' is not to say something about tame tigers but to say that there are tame tigers. Prof. G. E. Moore once brought out the difference between existence and a property such as that of being tame, or being a tiger, or being a growler, by reminding us that though the sentence 'some tame tigers do not *growl*' makes perfect sense, the sentence 'some tame tigers do not *exist*' has no clear meaning. The fundamental mistake in the ontological argument, then, is that it treats 'exists' in 'an infinitely perfect being exists' as if it ascribed a property existence to an infinitely perfect being, just as 'is loving' in 'an infinitely perfect being is loving' ascribes a property, or as 'growl' in 'tame tigers growl' ascribes a property: the verb 'to exist' in 'an infinitely perfect being exists' does not ascribe a property to something already conceived of as existing but says that the concept of an infinitely perfect being applies to something. The verb 'to exist' here takes us right out of the purely conceptual world. This being so, there can never be any *logical contradiction* in denying that God exists. It is worth mentioning that we are less likely to make the sort of mistake that the ontological argument makes if we use the expression 'there is a so-and-so' instead of the more misleading form of words 'a so-and-so exists'.

I should like to mention another interesting, though less crucial, objection to Descartes' argument. He talks as though you can deduce further properties of, say, a triangle, by considering its definition. It is worth pointing out that from the definition of a triangle as a figure bounded by three straight lines you can only deduce trivialities, such as that it is bounded by more than one straight line, for example. It is not at all a contradiction to say that the two sides of a triangle are together not greater than the third side, or that its angles do not add up to two right angles. To get a contradiction you have to bring in the specific axioms of Euclidean geometry. (Remember school geometry, how you used to prove that the angles of a triangle add up to two right angles. Through the vertex *C* of the triangle *ABC* you drew a line parallel to *BA*, and so you assumed the axiom of parallels for a start.) Definitions, by themselves, are not deductively potent. Descartes, though a very great mathematician himself, was profoundly mistaken as to the nature of mathematics. However, we can interpret him as saying that from the definition of a triangle, *together with the axioms of Euclidean geometry*, you can deduce various things, such as that the angles of a triangle add up to two right angles. But this just shows how pure mathematics is a sort of game with symbols; you start with a set of axioms, and operate on them in accordance with certain rules of inference. All the mathematician requires is that the axiom set should be *consistent*. Whether or not it has application to reality lies outside pure mathematics. Geometry is no fit model for a proof of real existence.

We now turn to the *Cosmological Argument*. This argument does at least seem more promising than the ontological argument. It does start with a factual premiss, namely that something exists. The premiss that something exists is indeed a very abstract one, but nevertheless it *is* factual, it does give us a foothold in the real world of things, it does go beyond the consideration of mere concepts. The argument has been put forward in various forms, but for present purposes it may be put as follows:

Everything in the world around us is *contingent*. That is, with regard to any particular thing, it is quite conceivable that it might not have existed. For example, if you were asked why you existed, you could say that it was because of your parents, and if asked why they existed you could go still further back, but however far you go back you have not, so it is argued, made the fact of your existence really intelligible. For however far back you go in such a series you only get back to something which itself might not have existed. For a really satisfying explanation of why anything contingent (such as you or me or this table) exists you must eventually begin with something which is not itself contingent, that is, with something of which we cannot say that it might not have existed, that is we must begin with a necessary being. So the first part of the argument boils down to this. *If anything exists an absolutely necessary being must exist. Something exists. Therefore an absolutely necessary being must exist.*

The second part of the argument is to prove that a necessarily existing being must be an infinitely perfect being, that is, God. Kant[2] contended that this second stage of the argument is just the ontological argument over again, and of course if this were so the cosmological argument would plainly be a fraud; it begins happily enough with an existential premiss ('something exists') but this would only be a cover for the subsequent employment of the ontological argument. This criticism of Kant's has been generally accepted but I think that certain Thomist philosophers have been right in attributing to Kant's own criticism a mistake in elementary logic. Let us look at Kant's criticism. Kant says, correctly enough, that the conclusion of the second stage of the cosmological argument is 'All necessarily existing beings are infinitely perfect beings'. This, he says implies that 'Some infinitely perfect beings are necessarily existing beings'. Since, however, there could be only one infinitely perfect, unlimited, being, we may replace the proposition 'Some infinitely perfect

[2] *Critique of Pure Reason*, A 603.

beings are necessarily existing beings' by the proposition 'All infinitely perfect beings are necessarily existing beings'. (To make this last point clearer let me take an analogous example. If it is true that some men who are Prime Minister of Australia are Liberals and if it is also true that there is only one Prime Minister of Australia, then we can equally well say that all men who are Prime Minister of Australia are Liberals. For 'some' means 'at least one', and if there is only one Prime Minister, then 'at least one' is equivalent to 'one', which in this case is 'all'.) So the conclusion of the second stage of the cosmological argument is that 'all infinitely perfect beings are necessarily existing beings'. This, however, is the principle of the ontological argument, which we have already criticized, and which, for that matter, proponents of the cosmological argument like Thomas Aquinas themselves reject.

Kant has, however, made a very simple mistake. He has forgotten that the existence of a necessary being has already been proved (or thought to have been proved) in the first part of the argument. He changes 'All necessary beings are infinitely perfect beings' round to 'Some infinitely perfect beings are necessary beings'. If this change round is to be valid the existence of a necessary being is already presupposed. Kant has been misled by an ambiguity in 'all'. 'All X's are Y's' may take it for granted that there are some X's or it may not. For example if I say, 'All the people in this room are interested in Philosophy', it is already agreed that there are some people in this room. So we can infer that 'Some of the people interested in Philosophy are people in this room'. So 'All the people in this room are interested in Philosophy' says more than 'If anyone were in this room he would be interested in

Philosophy', for this would be true even if there were in fact no people in this room. (As I wrote this lecture I was quite sure that *if* anyone came he would be interested in Philosophy, and I could have been quite sure of this even if I had doubted whether anyone would come.) Now sometimes 'All X's are Y's' does mean only 'If anything is an X it is a Y'. Take the sentence 'All trespassers will be prosecuted'. This does not imply that some prosecuted people will be trespassers, for it does not imply that there are or will be any trespassers. Indeed the object of putting it on a notice is to make it more likely that there won't be any trespassers. All that 'All trespassers will be prosecuted' says is, 'If anyone is a trespasser then he will be prosecuted'. So Kant's criticism won't do. He has taken himself and other people in by using 'all' sometimes in the one way and sometimes in the other.

While agreeing thus far with Thomist critics of Kant[3] I still want to assert that the cosmological argument is radically unsound. The trouble comes much earlier than where Kant locates it. The trouble comes in the *first* stage of the argument. For the first stage of the argument purports to argue to the existence of a necessary being. And by 'a necessary being' the cosmological argument means 'a *logically* necessary being', i.e. 'a being whose non-existence is inconceivable in the sort of way that a triangle's having four sides is inconceivable'. The trouble is, however, that the concept of a logically necessary being is a self-contradictory concept, like the concept of a round

[3] See, for example, Fr. T. A. Johnston, *Australasian Journal of Philosophy*, Vol. XXI (1943), pp. 14–15, or D. J. B. Hawkins, *Essentials of Theism* (New York, 1949), pp. 67–70, and the review of Fr. Hawkins' book by A. Donagan, *Australasian Journal of Philosophy*, Vol. XXVIII (1950), especially p. 129.

square. For in the first place 'necessary' is a predicate of *propositions*, not of things. That is, we can contrast *necessary* propositions such as '3 + 2 = 5', 'a thing cannot be red and green all over', 'either it is raining or it is not raining', with *contingent* propositions, such as 'Mr. Menzies is Prime Minister of Australia', 'the earth is slightly flattened at the poles', and 'sugar is soluble in water'. The propositions in the first class are guaranteed solely by the rules for the use of the symbols they contain. In the case of the propositions of the second class a genuine possibility of agreeing or not agreeing with reality is left open; whether they are true or false depends not on the conventions of our language but on reality. (Compare the contrast between 'the equator is 90 degrees from the pole', which tells us nothing about geography but only about our map-making conventions, and 'Adelaide is 55 degrees from the pole', which does tell us a geographical fact.) So no informative proposition can be logically necessary. Now since 'necessary' is a word which applies primarily to propositions, we shall have to interpret 'God is a necessary being' as 'The proposition "God exists" is logically necessary.' But this *is* the principle of the ontological argument, and there is no way of getting round it this time in the way that we got out of Kant's criticism. No existential proposition can be logically necessary, for we saw that the truth of a logically necessary proposition depends only on our symbolism, or to put the same thing in another way, on the relationship of concepts. We saw, however, in discussing the ontological argument, that an existential proposition does not say that one concept is involved in another, but that a concept applies to something. An existential proposition must be very different from any logically necessary one, such as a mathematical one, for example, for the conventions of our symbolism clearly leave it open for us either to affirm or deny an existential proposition; it is not our symbolism but reality which decides whether or not we must affirm it or deny it.

The demand that the existence of God should be *logically* necessary is thus a self-contradictory one. When we see this and go back to look at the first stage of the cosmological argument it no longer seems compelling, indeed it now seems to contain an absurdity. If we cast our minds back, we recall that the argument was as follows: that if we explain why something exists and is what it is, we must explain it by reference to something else, and we must explain that thing's being what it is by reference to yet another thing, and so on, back and back. It is then suggested that unless we can go back to a logically necessary first cause we shall remain intellectually unsatisfied. We should otherwise only get back to something which might have been otherwise, and with reference to which the same questions can again be asked. This is the argument, but we now see that in asking for a logically necessary first cause we are doing something worse than asking for the moon. It is only *physically* impossible for us to get the moon; if I were a few million times bigger I could reach out for it and give it to you. That is, I know what it would be *like* to give you the moon, though I cannot *in fact* do it. A logically necessary first cause, however, is not impossible in the way that giving you the moon is impossible; no, it is *logically* impossible. 'Logically necessary being' is a self-contradictory expression like 'round square'. It is not any good saying that we would only be intellectually satisfied with a logically necessary cause, that nothing else would do. We can easily have an absurd wish. We should all like to be able to eat our cake and have it, but that does not alter the fact that our wish is an absurd and self-contradictory one. We reject the cosmological argument, then, because it rests on a thorough absurdity.

Having reached this conclusion I should like to make one or two remarks about the necessity of God. First of all, I think that it is undeniable that if worship is to be what religion takes it to be, then God must be a necessary being in some sense or other of 'necessary'. He must not be just one of the things in the world, however big. To concede that he was just one of the things in the world, even a big one, would reduce religion to something near idolatry. All I wish to point out is that God can not be a *logically* necessary being, for the very supposition that he is is self-contradictory. (Hence, of course, to say that God is not logically necessary is not to place any limitations on him. It is not a limitation on your walking ability that you cannot go out of the room and not go out. To say that someone cannot do something self-contradictory is not to say that he is in any way impotent, it is to say that the sentence 'he did such and such and did not do it' is not a possible description of anything.) Theological necessity cannot be logical necessity. In the second place, I think I can see roughly what sort of necessity theological necessity might be. Let me give an analogy from physics. It is not a *logical* necessity that the velocity of light in a vacuum should be constant. It would, however, upset physical theory considerably if we denied it. Similarly it is not a logical necessity that God exists. But it would clearly upset the structure of our religious attitudes in the most violent way if we denied it or even entertained the possibility of its falsehood. So if we say that it is a *physical* necessity that the velocity of light *in vacuo* should be constant—(deny it and prevailing physical theory would have to be scrapped or at any rate drastically modified)—similarly we can say that it is a *religious* necessity that God exists. That is, we believe in the necessity of God's existence because we are Christians; we are not Christians because we believe in the necessity of God's existence. There are no short cuts to God. I draw your attention to the language of religion itself, where we talk of *conversion*, not of *proof*. In my opinion religion can stand on its own feet, but to found it on a metaphysical argument *a priori* is to found it on absurdity born of ignorance of the logic of our language. I am reminded of what was said about the Boyle lectures in the eighteenth century: that no one doubted that God existed until the Boyle lecturers started to prove it.

Perhaps now is the time to say why I suggested at the beginning of the lecture that 'Does God exist?' is not a proper question. Once again I make use of an analogy from science. 'Do electrons exist?' (asked just like that) is not a proper question. In order to acquire the concept of an electron we must find out about experiments with cathode-ray tubes, the Wilson cloud chamber, about spectra and so on. We then find the concept of the electron a useful one, one which plays a part in a mass of physical theory. When we reach this stage the question 'Do electrons exist?' no longer arises. Before we reached this stage the question 'Do electrons exist?' had no clear meaning. Similarly, I suggest, the question 'Does God exist?' has no clear meaning for the unconverted. But for the converted the question no longer arises. The word 'God' gets its meaning from the part it plays in religious speech and literature, and in religious speech and literature the question of existence does not arise. A theological professor at Glasgow once said to me: 'Religion is "O God, if you exist, save my soul if it exists!"' This of course was a joke. It clearly is just *not* what religion is. So within religion the question 'Does God exist?' does not arise, any more than the question 'Do electrons exist?' arises within physics. Outside religion the question 'Does God exist?' has as little meaning as the question 'Do electrons exist?' as asked by the scientifically ignorant. Thus I suggest that it is possible to hold that the question 'Does God exist?' is not a proper question without necessarily also holding that religion and theology are nonsensical.

The cosmological argument, we saw, failed because it made use of the absurd conception of a *logically* necessary being. We now pass to the third argument which I propose to consider. This is the *Teleological Argument*. It is also called 'the Argument from Design'. It would be better called the argument *to* design, as Kemp Smith does call it, for clearly that the universe has been designed by a great architect is to assume a great part of the conclusion to be proved. Or we could call it 'the argument from apparent design'. The argument is very fully discussed in Hume's *Dialogues concerning Natural Religion*, to which I should like to draw your attention. In these dialogues the argument is presented as follows:

> Look round the world: Contemplate the whole and every part of it: You will find it to be nothing but one great machine, subdivided into an infinite number of lesser machines. . . . The curious adapting of means to ends, throughout all nature, resembles exactly, though it much exceeds, the productions of human contrivance. . . . Since therefore the effects resemble each other, we are led to infer, by all the rules

of analogy, that the causes also resemble; and that the Author of nature is somewhat similar to the mind of man; though possessed of much larger faculties, proportioned to the grandeur of the work which he has executed.

This argument may at once be criticized in two ways: (1) We may question whether the analogy between the universe and artificial things like houses, ships, furniture, and machines (which admittedly are designed) is very close. Now in any ordinary sense of language, it is true to say that plants and animals have *not* been designed. If we press the analogy of the universe to a plant, instead of to a machine, we get to a very different conclusion. And why should the one analogy be regarded as any better or worse than the other? (2) Even if the analogy were close, it would only go to suggest that the universe was designed by a *very great* (not infinite) architect, and note, an *architect*, not a *creator*. For if we take the analogy seriously we must notice that we do not create the materials from which we make houses, machines and so on, but only *arrange* the materials.

This, in bare outline, is the general objection to the argument from design, and will apply to any form of it. In the form in which the argument was put forward by such theologians as Paley, the argument is, of course, still more open to objection. For Paley laid special stress on such things as the eye of an animal, which he thought must have been contrived by a wise Creator for the special benefit of the animal. It seemed to him inconceivable how otherwise such a complex organ, so well suited to the needs of the animal, should have arisen. Or listen to Henry More:

> For why have we three joints in our legs and arms, as also in our fingers, but that it was much better than

having two or four? And why are our fore-teeth sharp like chisels to cut, but our inward teeth broad to grind, [instead of] the fore-teeth broad and the other sharp? But we might have made a hard shift to have lived through in that worser condition. Again, why are the teeth so luckily placed, or rather, why are there not teeth in other bones as well as in the jaw-bones? for they might have been as capable as these. But the reason is, nothing is done foolishly or in vain; that is, there is a divine Providence that orders all things.

This type of argument has lost its persuasiveness, for the theory of Evolution explains why our teeth are so luckily placed in our jaw-bones, why we have the most convenient number of joints in our fingers, and so on. Species which did not possess advantageous features would not survive in competition with those which did.

The sort of argument Paley and Henry More used is thus quite unconvincing. Let us return to the broader conception, that of the universe as a whole, which seems to show the mark of a benevolent and intelligent Designer. Bacon expressed this belief forcibly: 'I had rather beleave all the Fables in the Legend and the Talmud and the Alcoran than that this Universal Frame is without a Minde.' So, in some moods, does the universe strike us. But sometimes, when we are in other moods, we see it very differently. To quote Hume's dialogues again:

Look around this Universe. What an immense profusion of beings, animated and organized, sensible and active! You admire this prodigious variety and fecundity. But inspect a little more narrowly these living existences, the only beings worth regarding. How hostile and destructive to each other! How insufficient all of them for their own happiness! . . . the whole presents nothing but the idea of a blind Nature, impregnated by a great vivifying principle, and pouring forth from her lap, without discernment or parental care, her maimed and abortive children!

There is indeed a great deal of suffering, some part of which is no doubt attributable to the moral choices of men, and to save us from which would conflict with what many people would regard as the greater good of moral freedom, but there is still an immense residue of apparently needless suffering, that is, needless in the sense that it could be prevented by an omnipotent being. The difficulty is that of reconciling the presence of evil and suffering with the assertion that God is both omnipotent and benevolent. If we *already* believe in an omnipotent and benevolent God, then some attempt may be made to solve the problem of evil by arguing that the values in the world form a sort of organic unity, and that making any *part* of the world better would perhaps nevertheless reduce the value of the whole. Paradoxical though this thesis may appear at first sight, it is perhaps not theoretically absurd. If, however, evil presents a *difficulty* to the believing mind, it presents an *insuperable* difficulty to one who wishes to argue rationally from the world as we find it to the existence of an omnipotent and benevolent God. As Hume puts it:

> Is the world considered in general, and as it appears to us in this life, different from what a man . . . would *beforehand* expect from a very powerful, wise and benevolent Deity? It must be a strange prejudice to assert the contrary. And from thence I conclude, that, however consistent the world may be, allowing certain suppositions and conjectures, with the idea of such a Deity, it can never afford us an inference concerning his existence.

The teleological argument is thus extremely shaky, and in any case, even if it were sound, it would only go to prove the existence of a very great architect, not of an omnipotent and benevolent Creator.

Nevertheless, the argument has a fascination for us that reason can not easily dispel. Hume, in his twelfth dialogue, and after pulling the argument from design to pieces in the previous eleven dialogues, nevertheless speaks as follows:

> A purpose, an intention, a design strikes everywhere the most careless, the most stupid thinker; and no man can be so hardened in absurd systems as at all times to reject it . . . all the sciences almost lead us insensibly to acknowledge a first Author.

Similarly Kant, before going on to exhibit the fallaciousness of the argument, nevertheless says of it:

> This proof always deserves to be mentioned with respect. It is the oldest, the clearest and the most accordant with the common reason of mankind. It enlivens the study of nature, just as it itself derives its existence and gains ever new vigour from that source. It suggests ends and purposes, where our observation would not have detected them by itself, and extends our knowledge of nature by means of the guiding-concept of a special unity, the principle of which is outside nature. This knowledge . . . so strengthens the belief in a supreme Author of nature that the belief acquires the force of an irresistible conviction.

It is somewhat of a paradox that an invalid argument should command so much respect even from those who have demonstrated its invalidity. The solution of the paradox is perhaps somewhat as follows[4]: The

[4] See also N. Kemp Smith's Henrietta Hertz Lecture, "Is Divine Existence Credible?" *Proceedings of the British Academy* (1931).

argument from design is no good as an argument. But in those who have the seeds of a genuinely religious attitude already within them the facts to which the argument from design draws attention, facts showing the grandeur and majesty of the universe, facts that are evident to anyone who looks upwards on a starry night, and which are enormously multiplied for us by the advance of theoretical science, these facts have a powerful effect. But they only have this effect on the already religious mind, on the mind which has the capability of feeling the religious type of awe. That is, the argument from design is in reality no argument, or if it is regarded as an argument it is feeble, but it is a potent instrument in heightening religious emotions.

Something similar might even be said of the cosmological argument. As an argument it cannot pass muster at all; indeed it is completely absurd, as employing the notion of a logically necessary being. Nevertheless it does appeal to something deep seated in our natures. It takes its stand on the fact that the existence of you or me or this table is not logically necessary. Logic tells us that this fact is not a fact at all, but is a truism, like the 'fact' that a circle is not a square. Again, the cosmological argument tries to base the existence of you or me or this table on the existence of a logically necessary being, and hence commits a rank absurdity, the notion of a logically necessary being being self-contradictory. So the only rational thing to say if someone asks 'Why does this table exist?' is some such thing as that such and such a carpenter made it. We can go back and back in such a series, but we must not entertain the absurd idea of getting back to something logically necessary. However, now let us ask, 'Why should anything exist at all?' Logic seems to tell us that the only answer which is not absurd is to say, 'Why shouldn't it?' Nevertheless, though I know how any answer on the lines of the cosmological argument can be pulled to pieces by a correct logic, I still feel I want to go on asking the question. Indeed, though logic has taught me to look at such a question with the gravest suspicion, my mind often seems to reel under the immense significance it seems to have for me. That anything should exist at all does seem to me a matter for the deepest awe. But whether other people feel this sort of awe, and whether they or I ought to is another question. I think we ought to. If so, the question arises: If 'Why should anything exist at all?' cannot be interpreted after the manner of the cosmological argument, that is, as an absurd request for the nonsensical postulation of a logically necessary being, what sort of question is it? What sort of question is this question 'Why should anything exist at all?' All I can say is, that I do not yet know.

B. RICHARD TAYLOR (1919–)

[Richard Taylor is a member of the philosophy department at the University of Rochester. At issue in the present article is the relationship of metaphysics to God. Professor Taylor contends that metaphysical questions are a legitimate part of reason, even though few people are aware that their assertions are often metaphysical. Thinking, in all but its most provincial aspect, stimulates numerous metaphysical issues; it involves, for example, the principle of sufficient reason, which in turn involves questions concerning necessary and contingent truth. Professor Taylor's essay raises such metaphysical issues and proceeds to analyze them in provocative fashion. For instance, if it is admitted that there is a rational explanation for everything, then may not an explanation for the universe itself be sought? And if so, must the universe be regarded as being without beginning rather than as having a beginning?]

Metaphysics and God*

An active, living, and religious belief in the gods has probably never arisen and been maintained on purely metaphysical grounds. Such beliefs are found in every civilized land and time, and are often virtually universal in a particular culture, yet relatively few men have

*From *Metaphysics* (Englewood Cliffs, N. J., 1963). © 1963. Reprinted by permission of Prentice-Hall, Inc.

much of a conception of metaphysics. There are in fact entire cultures, such as ancient Israel, to whom metaphysics is quite foreign, though these cultures may nevertheless be religious.

Belief in the gods seems to have its roots in human desires and fears, particularly those associated with self-preservation. Like all other creatures, men have a profound will to live, which is what mainly gives one's existence a meaning from one sunrise to the next. Unlike other creatures, however, men are capable of the full and terrible realization of their own inevitable decay. A man can bring before his mind the image of his own grave, and with it the complete certainty of its ultimate reality, and against this his will naturally recoils. It can hardly seem to him less than an absolute catastrophe, the very end, so far as he is concerned, of everything, though he has no difficulty viewing death, as it touches others more or less remote from himself, as a perhaps puzzling, occasionally distressing, but nonetheless necessary aspect of nature. It is probably partly in response to this fear that he turns to the gods, as those beings of such power that they can overturn this verdict of nature.

The sources of religious belief are doubtless much more complex than this, but they seem to lie in man's will rather than in his speculative intelligence, nevertheless. Men who possess such a belief seldom permit any metaphysical considerations to wrest it from them, while those who lack it are seldom turned toward it by other metaphysical considerations. Still, in every land in which philosophy has flourished, there have been profound thinkers who have sought to discover some metaphysical basis for a rational belief in the existence of some supreme being or beings. Even though religion may properly be a matter of faith rather than reason, still, a philosophical person can hardly help wondering whether it might, at least in part, be also a matter of reason, and whether, in particular, the existence of God might be something that can be not merely believed but shown. It is this question that we want now to consider; that is, we want to see whether there are not strong metaphysical considerations from which the existence of some supreme and supranatural being might reasonably be inferred.

Suppose you were strolling in the woods and, in addition to the sticks, stones, and other accustomed litter of the forest floor, you one day came upon some quite unaccustomed object, something not quite like what you had ever seen before and would never expect to find in such a place. Suppose, for example, that it is a large ball, about your own height, perfectly smooth and translucent. You would deem this puzzling and mysterious, certainly, but if one considers the matter, it is no more inherently mysterious that such a thing should exist than that anything else should exist. If you were quite accustomed to finding such objects of various sizes around you most of the time, but had never seen an ordinary rock, then upon finding a large rock in the woods one day you would be just as puzzled and mystified. This illustrates the fact that something that is mysterious ceases to seem so simply by its accustomed presence. It is strange indeed, for example, that a world such as ours should exist; yet few men are very often struck by this strangeness, but simply take it for granted.

Suppose, then, that you have found this translucent ball and are mystified by it. Now whatever else you might wonder about it, there is one thing you would hardly question; namely, that it did not appear there all by itself, that it owes its existence to something.

You might not have the remotest idea whence and how it came to be there, but you would hardly doubt that there was an explanation. The idea that it might have come from nothing at all, that it might exist without there being any explanation of its existence, is one that few people would consider worthy of entertaining.

This illustrates a metaphysical belief that seems to be almost a part of reason itself, even though few men ever think upon it; the belief, namely, that there is some explanation for the existence of anything whatever, some reason why it should exist rather than not. The sheer nonexistence of anything, which is not to be confused with the passing out of existence of something, never requires a reason; but existence does. That there should never have been any such ball in the forest does not require any explanation or reason, but that there should ever be such a ball does. If one were to look upon a barren plain and ask why there is not and never has been any large translucent ball there, the natural response would be to ask why there should be; but if one finds such a ball, and wonders why it is there, it is not quite so natural to ask why it should *not* be, as though existence should simply be taken for granted. That anything should not exist, then, and that, for instance, no such ball should exist in the forest, or that there should be no forest for it to occupy, or no continent containing a forest, or no earth, nor any world at all, do not seem to be things for which there needs to be any explanation or reason; but that such things should be, does seem to require a reason.

The principle involved here has been called the principle of sufficient reason. Actually, it is a very general principle, and is best expressed by saying that, in the case of any positive truth, there is some sufficient reason for it, something which, in this sense, makes it true—in short, that there is some sort of explanation, known or unknown, for everything.

Now some truths depend on something else, and are accordingly called *contingent*, while others depend only upon themselves, that is, are true by their very natures and are accordingly called *necessary*. There is, for example, a reason why the stone on my window sill is warm; namely, that the sun is shining upon it. This happens to be true, but not by its very nature. Hence, it is contingent, and depends upon something other than itself. It is also true that all the points of a circle are equidistant from the center, but this truth depends upon nothing but itself. No matter what happens, nothing can make it false. Similarly, it is a truth, and a necessary one, that if the stone on my window sill is a body, as it is, then it has a form, since this fact depends upon nothing but itself for its confirmation. Untruths are also, of course, either contingent or necessary, it being contingently false, for example, that the stone on my window sill is cold, and necessarily false that it is both a body and formless, since this is by its very nature impossible.

The principle of sufficient reason can be illustrated in various ways, as we have done, and if one thinks about it, he is apt to find that he presupposes it in his thinking about reality, but it cannot be proved. It does not appear to be itself a necessary truth, and at the same time it would be most odd to say it is contingent. If one were to try proving it, he would sooner or later have to appeal to considerations that are less plausible than the principle itself. Indeed, it is hard to see how one could even make an argument for it, without already assuming it. For this reason it might properly be called a presupposition of reason itself. One can deny that it is true, without embarrassment or fear of refutation, but one is then apt to find that what he is denying is not really what the principle asserts. We shall, then, treat it here as a datum—not something that is provably true, but as something which all men, whether they ever reflect upon it or not, seem more or less to presuppose.

It happens to be true that something exists, that there is, for example, a world, and while no one ever seriously supposes that this might not be so, that there might exist nothing at all, there still seems to be nothing the least necessary in this, considering it just by itself. That no world should ever exist at all is perfectly comprehensible and seems to express not the slightest absurdity. Considering any particular item in the world it seems not at all necessary in itself that it should ever have existed, nor does it appear any more necessary that the totality of these things, or any totality of things, should ever exist.

From the principle of sufficient reason it follows, of course, that there must be a reason, not only for the existence of everything in the world but for the world itself, meaning by "the world" simply everything that ever does exist, except God, in case there is a god. This principle does not imply that there must be some purpose or goal for everything, or for the totality of all things; for explanations need not, and in fact seldom are, teleological or purposeful. All the principle requires is that there be some sort of reason for everything. And it would certainly be odd to maintain that everything in the world owes its existence to something, that nothing in the world is either purely accidental, or such that it just bestows its own being upon itself, and then to deny this of the world itself. One can indeed *say* that the world is in some sense a pure accident, that there simply is no reason at all why this or any world should exist, and one can equally say that the world exists by its very nature, or is an inherently necessary being. But it is at least very odd and arbitrary to deny of this existing world the need for any sufficient reason, whether independent of itself or not, while presupposing that there is a reason for every other thing that ever exists.

Consider again the strange ball that we imagine has been found in the forest. Now we can hardly doubt that there must be an explanation for the existence of such a thing, though we may have no notion what that explanation is. It is not, moreover, the fact of its having been found in the forest rather than elsewhere that renders an explanation necessary. It matters not in the least where it happens to be, for our question is not how it happens to be *there* but how it happens to exist at all. If we in our imagination annihilate the forest, leaving only this ball in an open field, our conviction that it is a contingent thing and owes its existence to something other than itself is not reduced in the least. If we now imagine the field to be annihilated, and in fact everything else as well to vanish into nothingness, leaving only this ball to constitute the entire physical universe, then we cannot for a moment suppose that its existence has thereby been explained, or the need of any explanation eliminated, or that its existence is suddenly rendered self-explanatory. If we now carry this thought one step further and suppose that no other reality ever has existed or ever will exist, that this ball forever constitutes the entire physical universe, then we must still insist on there being some reason independent of itself why it should exist rather than not. If there must be a reason for the existence of any particular thing, then the necessity of such a reason is not eliminated by the mere supposition that certain other things do *not* exist. And again, it matters not at all what the thing in question is, whether it be large and complex, such as the world we actually find ourselves in, or whether it be something small, simple and insignificant, such as a ball, a bacterium, or the merest grain of sand. We do not avoid the necessity of a reason for the existence of something merely by describing it in this way or that. And it would, in any event, seem quite plainly absurd to say that if the world were comprised entirely of a single ball about six feet in diameter, or of a single grain of sand, then it would be contingent and there would have to be some explanation other than itself why such a thing exists, but that, since the actual world is vastly more complex than this, there is no need for an explanation of its existence, independent of itself.

It should now be noted that it is no answer to the question, why a thing exists, to state *how long* it has existed. A geologist does not suppose that he has explained why there should be rivers and mountains merely by pointing out that they are old. Similarly, if one were to ask, concerning the ball of which we have spoken, for some sufficient reason for its being, he would not receive any answer upon being told that it had been there since yesterday. Nor would it be any better answer to say that it had existed since before anyone could remember, or even that it had always existed; for the question was not one concerning its age but its existence. If, to be sure, one were to ask where a given thing came from, or how it came into being, then upon learning that it had always existed he would learn that it never really *came* into being at all; but he could still reasonably wonder why it should exist at all. If, accordingly, the world—that is, the totality of all things excepting God, in case there is a god—had really no beginning at all, but has always existed in some form or other, then there is clearly no answer to the question, where it came from and when; it did not, on this supposition, *come* from anything at all, at any time. But still, it can be asked why there is a world, why indeed there is a beginningless world, why there should have perhaps always been something rather than nothing. And, if the principle of sufficient reason is a good principle, there must be an answer to that question, an answer that is by no means supplied by giving the world an age, or even an infinite age.

This brings out an important point with respect to the concept of creation that is often misunderstood, particularly by those whose thinking has been influenced by Christian ideas. People tend to think that creation—for example, the creation of the world by God—*means* creation *in time*, from which it of course logically follows that if the world had no beginning in time, then it cannot be the creation of God. This, however, is erroneous, for creation means essentially *dependence*, even in Christian theology. If one thing is the creation of another, then it depends for its existence on that other, and this is perfectly consistent with saying that both are eternal, that neither ever came into being, and hence, that neither was ever created at any point of time. Perhaps an analogy will help convey this point. Consider, then, a flame that is casting beams of light. Now there seems to be a clear sense in which the beams of light are dependent for their existence upon the flame, which is their source, while the flame, on the other hand, is not similarly dependent for its existence upon them. The beams of light arise from the flame, but the flame does not arise from them. In this sense, they are the creation of the flame; they derive their existence from it. And none of this has

any reference to time; the relationship of dependence
in such a case would not be altered in the slightest if
we supposed that the flame, and with it the beams of
light, had always existed, that neither had ever *come*
into being.

Now if the world is the creation of God, its relationship to God should be thought of in this fashion;
namely, that the world depends for its existence upon
God, and could not exist independently of God. If God
is eternal, as those who believe in God generally assume, then the world may (though it need not) be
eternal too, without that altering in the least its dependence upon God for its existence, and hence without altering its being the creation of God. The supposition of God's eternality, on the other hand, does not
by itself imply that the world is eternal too; for there
is not the least reason why something of finite duration might not depend for its existence upon something
of infinite duration—though the reverse is, of course,
impossible.

If we think of God as "the creator of heaven and
earth," and if we consider heaven and earth to include
everything that exists except God, then we appear to
have, in the foregoing considerations, fairly strong reasons for asserting that God, as so conceived, exists.
Now of course most people have much more in mind
than this when they think of God, for religions have
ascribed to God ever so many attributes that are not
at all implied by describing him merely as the creator
of the world; but that is not relevant here. Most religious persons do, in any case, think of God as being
at least the creator, as that being upon which everything ultimately depends, no matter what else they may
say about him in addition. It is, in fact, the first item
in the creeds of Christianity that God is the "creator

of heaven and earth." And, it seems, there are good metaphysical reasons, as distinguished from the persuasions of faith, for thinking that such a creative being exists.

If, as seems clearly implied by the principle of sufficient reason, there must be a reason for the existence of heaven and earth—i.e., for the world—then that reason must be found either in the world itself, or outside it, in something that is literally supranatural, or outside heaven and earth. Now if we suppose that the world—i.e., the totality of all things except God—contains within itself the reason for its existence, we are supposing that it exists by its very nature, that is, that it is a necessary being. In that case there would, of course, be no reason for saying that it must depend upon God or anything else for its existence; for if it exists by its very nature, then it depends upon nothing but itself, much as the sun depends upon nothing but itself for its heat. This, however, is implausible, for we find nothing about the world or anything in it to suggest that it exists by its own nature, and we do find, on the contrary, ever so many things to suggest that it does not. For in the first place, anything which exists by its very nature must necessarily be eternal and indestructible. It would be a self-contradiction to say of anything that it exists by its own nature, or is a necessarily existing thing, and at the same time to say that it comes into being or passes away, or that it ever could come into being or pass away. Nothing about the world seems at all like this, for concerning anything in the world, we can perfectly easily think of it as being annihilated, or as never having existed in the first place, without there being the slightest hint of any absurdity in such a supposition. Some of the things in the universe are, to be sure, very old; the moon, for example, or the stars and the planets. It is even possible to imagine that they have always existed. Yet it seems quite impossible to suppose that they owe their existence to nothing but themselves, that they bestow existence upon themselves by their very natures, or that they are in themselves things of such nature that it would be impossible for them not to exist. Even if we suppose that something, such as the sun, for instance, has existed forever, and will never cease, still we cannot conclude just from this that it exists by its own nature. If, as is of course very doubtful, the sun has existed forever and will never cease, then it is possible that its heat and light have also existed forever and will never cease; but that would not show that the heat and light of the sun exist by their own natures. They are obviously contingent and depend on the sun for their existence, whether they are beginningless and everlasting or not.

There seems to be nothing in the world, then, concerning which it is at all plausible to suppose that it exists by its own nature, or contains within itself the reason for its existence. In fact, everything in the world appears to be quite plainly the opposite, namely, something that not only need not exist, but at some time or other, past or future or both, does not in fact exist. Everything in the world seems to have a finite duration, whether long or short. Most things, such as ourselves, exist only for a short while; they come into being, then soon cease. Other things, like the heavenly bodies, last longer, but they are still corruptible, and from all that we can gather about them, they too seem destined eventually to perish. We arrive at the conclusion, then, that while the world may contain some things which have always existed and are destined never to perish, it is nevertheless doubtful that it contains any such thing and, in any case, everything in the world is capable of perishing, and nothing in it, however long it may already have existed and however long it may yet remain, exists by its own nature, but depends instead upon something else.

While this might be true of everything in the world, is it necessarily true of the world itself? That is, if we grant, as we seem forced to, that nothing in the world exists by its own nature, that everything in the world is contingent and perishable, must we also say that the world itself, or the totality of all these perishable things, is also contingent and perishable? Logically, we are not forced to, for it is logically possible that the totality of all perishable things might itself be imperishable, and hence, that the world might exist by its own nature, even though it is comprised exclusively of things which are contingent. It is not logically necessary that a totality should share the defects of its members. For example, even though every man is mortal, it does not follow from this that the human race, or the totality of all men, is also mortal; for it is possible that there will always be human beings, even though there are no human beings which will always exist. Similarly, it is possible that the world is in itself a necessary thing, even though it is comprised entirely of things that are contingent.

This is logically possible, but it is not plausible. For we find nothing whatever about the world, any more than in its parts, to suggest that it exists by its own nature. Concerning anything in the world, we have not the slightest difficulty in supposing that it should perish, or even, that it should never have existed in the first place. We have almost as little difficulty in supposing this of the world itself. It might be somewhat hard to think of everything as utterly perishing and leaving no trace whatever of its ever having been, but there seems to be not the slightest difficulty in imagining that the world should never have existed in the first place. We can, for instance, perfectly easily suppose that nothing in the world had ever existed except, let us suppose, a single grain of sand, and we can thus suppose that this grain of sand has forever constituted the whole universe. Now if we consider just this grain of sand, it is quite impossible for us to suppose that it exists by its very nature, and could never have failed to exist. It clearly depends for its existence upon something other than itself, if it depends on anything at all. The same will be true if we consider the world to consist, not of one grain of sand, but of two, or of a million, or, as we in fact find, of a vast number of stars and planets and all their minuter parts.

It would seem, then, that the world, in case it happens to exist at all—and this is quite beyond doubt— is contingent and thus dependent upon something other than itself for its existence, if it depends upon anything at all. And it must depend upon something, for otherwise there could be no reason why it exists in the first place. Now that upon which the world depends must be something that either exists by its own nature or does not. If it does not exist by its own nature, then it, in turn, depends for its existence upon something else, and so on. Now then, we can say either of two things; namely, (1) that the world depends for its existence upon something else, which in turn depends on still another thing, this depending upon still another, *ad infinitum*; or (2) that the world derives its existence from something that exists by its own nature and which is accordingly eternal and imperishable, and is the creator of heaven and earth. The first of these alternatives, however, is impossible, for it does not render a sufficient reason why anything should exist in the first place. Instead of supplying a reason why any world should exist, it repeatedly begs off giving a reason. It explains what is dependent and perishable in terms of what is itself dependent and perishable, leaving us still without a reason why perishable things should exist at all, which is what we are seeking. Ultimately, then, it would seem that the world, or the totality of contingent or perishable things, in case it exists at all, must depend upon something that is necessary and imperishable, and which accordingly exists, not in dependence upon something else, but by its own nature.

What has been said thus far gives some intimation of what meaning should be attached to the concept of a self-caused being, a concept that is quite generally misunderstood, sometimes even by scholars. To say that something—God, for example—is self-caused, or is the cause of its own existence, does not mean that this being brings itself into existence, which is a perfectly absurd idea. Nothing can *bring* itself into existence. To say that something is self-caused (*causa sui*) means only that it exists, not contingently or in dependence upon something else, but by its own nature, which is only to say that it is a being which is such that it can neither come into being nor perish. Now whether such a being in fact exists or not, there is in any case no absurdity in the idea. We have found, in fact, that the principle of sufficient reason seems to point to the existence of such a being, as that upon which the world, with everything in it, must ultimately depend for its existence.

A being that depends for its existence upon nothing but itself, and is in this sense self-caused, can equally be described as a necessary being; that is to say, a being that is not contingent, and hence not perishable. For in the case of anything which exists by its own nature, and is dependent upon nothing else, it is impossible that it should not exist, which is equivalent to saying that it is necessary. Many persons have professed to find the gravest difficulties in this concept, too, but that is partly because it has been confused with other notions. If it makes sense to speak of anything as an *impossible* being, or something which by its very nature does not exist, then it is hard to see why the idea of a necessary being, or something which in its very nature exists, should not be just as comprehensible. And of course, we have not the slightest difficulty in speaking of something, such as a square circle or a formless body, as an impossible being. And if it makes sense to speak of something as being perishable, contingent, and dependent upon something other than itself for its existence, as it surely does, then there seems to be no difficulty in thinking of something as imperishable and dependent upon nothing other than itself for its existence.

From these considerations we can see also what is properly meant by a first cause, an appellative that has often been applied to God by theologians, and which many persons have deemed an absurdity. It is a common criticism of this notion to say that there need not be any first cause, since the series of causes and effects which constitute the history of the universe might be infinite or beginningless and must, in fact, be infinite in case the universe itself had no beginning in time. This criticism, however, reflects a total misconception of what is meant by a first cause. *First* here does not mean first in time, and when God is spoken of as a first cause, he is not being described as a being which, at some time in the remote past, *started* everything. To describe God as a first cause is only to say that he is literally a *primary* rather than a secondary cause, an *ultimate* rather than a derived cause, or a being upon which all other things, heaven and earth, ultimately depend for their existence. It is, in short, only to say that God is the creator, in the sense of creation explained above. Now this, of course, is perfectly consistent with saying that the world is eternal or beginningless. As we have seen, one gives no reason for the existence of a world merely by giving it an age, even if it is supposed to have an infinite age. To use a helpful analogy, we can say that the sun is the first cause of daylight and, for that matter, of the moonlight of the night as well, which means only that daylight and moonlight ultimately depend upon the sun for their existence. The moon, on the other hand, is only a secondary or derivative cause of its light. This light would be no less dependent upon the sun if we affirmed that it had no beginning, for an ageless and beginningless light requires a source no less than an ephemeral one. If we supposed that the sun has always existed, and with it its light, then we would have to say that the sun has always been the first—i.e., the primary or ultimate—cause of its light. Such is precisely the manner in which God should be thought of, and is by theologians often thought of, as the first cause of heaven and earth.

C. PAUL TILLICH (1886–1966)

[It is impossible to survey contemporary philosophical
theology without recognizing Paul Tillich's influence.
His entire intellectual life was spent in an interpreta-
tive liaison between philosophy and theology. In this
brief passage, one can barely sample his position. He
begins by insisting that men must ask the cosmological
questions because such issues are attached to the
ground of man's nature. Tillich holds no hope, however, that such questions can be resolved. Reason will
not stretch into infinity. The questions carry symbolic
significance but also clearly reveal the inadequacy of
reason as an ultimate religious solution. Rational
agnosticism makes room for revelatory (psycho-
mystical) experience.]

The Question of God*

The question of God *can* be asked because there is
an unconditional element in the very act of asking any
question. The question of God *must* be asked because
the threat of nonbeing, which man experiences as anxiety, drives him to the question of being conquering
nonbeing and of courage conquering anxiety. This
question is the cosmological question of God.

The so-called cosmological and teleological argu-

* From *Systematic Theology,* Vol. I (Chicago, 1951). Copy-
right 1951 by The University of Chicago. Reprinted by per-
printed by permission of The University of Chicago Press.

ments for the existence of God are the traditional and inadequate form of this question. In all their variations these arguments move from special characteristics of the world to the existence of a highest being. They are valid in so far as they give an analysis of reality which indicates that the cosmological question of God is unavoidable. They are not valid in so far as they claim that the existence of a highest being is the logical conclusion of their analysis, which is as impossible logically, as it is impossible existentially to derive courage from anxiety.

The cosmological method of arguing for the existence of God has taken two main paths. It has moved from the finitude of being to an infinite being (the cosmological argument in the narrower sense), and it has moved from the finitude of meaning to a bearer of infinite meaning (the teleological argument in the traditional sense). In both cases the cosmological question comes out of the element of nonbeing in beings and meanings. No question of God would arise if there were no logical and noological (relating to meaning) threat of nonbeing, for then being would be safe; religiously speaking, God would be present in it.

The first form of the cosmological argument is determined by the categorical structure of finitude. From the endless chain of causes and effects it arrives at the conclusion that there is a first cause, and from the contingency of all substances it concludes that there is a necessary substance. But cause and substance are categories of finitude. The "first cause" is a hypostasized question, not a statement about a being which initiates the causal chain. Such a being would itself be a part of the causal chain and would again raise the question of cause. In the same way, a "necessary substance" is a hypostasized question, not a statement about a being which gives substantiality to all substances. Such a being would itself be a substance with accidents and would again open the question of substantiality itself. When used as material for "arguments," both categories lose their categorical character. First cause and necessary substance are symbols which express the question implied in finite being, the question of that which transcends finitude and categories, the question of being-itself embracing and conquering nonbeing, the question of God.

The cosmological question of God is the question about that which ultimately makes courage possible, a courage which accepts and overcomes the anxiety of categorical finitude. We have analyzed the labile balance between anxiety and courage in relation to time, space, causality, and substance. In each case we finally have come face to face with the question how the courage which resists the threat of nonbeing implied in these categories is possible. Finite being includes courage, but it cannot maintain courage against the ultimate threat of nonbeing. It needs a basis for ultimate courage. Finite being is a question mark. It asks the question of the "eternal now" in which the temporal and the spatial are simultaneously accepted and overcome. It asks the question of the "ground of being" in which the causal and the substantial are simultaneously confirmed and negated. The cosmological approach cannot answer these questions, but it can and it must analyze their roots in the structure of finitude.

The basis for the so-called teleological argument for the existence of God is the threat against the finite structure of being, that is, against the unity of its polar elements. The *telos,* from which this argument has received its name, is the "inner aim," the meaningful, understandable structure of reality. This structure is used as a springboard to the conclusion that finite *teloi* imply an infinite cause of teleology, that finite and threatened meanings imply an infinite and unthreatened cause of meaning. In terms of logical argument this conclusion is as invalid as the other cosmological "arguments." As the statement of a question it is not only valid but inescapable and, as history shows, most impressive. Anxiety about meaninglessness is the characteristically *human* form of ontological anxiety. It is the form of anxiety which only a being can have in whose nature freedom and destiny are united. The threat of losing this unity drives man toward the question of an infinite, unthreatened ground of meaning; it drives him to the question of God. The teleological argument formulates the question of the ground of meaning, just as the cosmological argument formulates the question of the ground of being. In contrast to the ontological argument, however, both are in the larger sense cosmological and stand over against it.

The task of a theological treatment of the traditional arguments for the existence of God is twofold: to develop the question of God which they express and to expose the impotency of the "arguments," their inability to answer the question of God. These arguments bring the ontological analysis to a conclusion by disclosing that the question of God is implied in the finite structure of being. In performing this function, they partially accept and also partially reject traditional natural theology, and they drive reason to the quest for revelation.

SELECTED BIBLIOGRAPHY

Clark, Robert E. D. *The Universe: Plan or Accident?* Philadelphia: Muhlenberg Press, 1961.

Copleston, F. C. *Aquinas*. London: Penguin Books, 1955.

Daniélou, Jean. *God and the Ways of Knowing*. New York: Meridian Books, Inc., 1957. Chapter 2.

Ewing, A. C. *The Fundamental Questions of Philosophy*. New York: The Macmillan Company, 1951.

Farrer, Austin. *Finite and Infinite*. London: Dacre Press, 1943.

———. *Love Almighty and Ills Unlimited*. New York: Doubleday & Co., Inc., 1961.

Flew, Antony. *God and Philosophy*. London: Hutchinson & Co., 1966.

———. *Hume's Philosophy of Belief*. London: Routledge & Kegan Paul, 1961.

Garrigou-Lagrange, R. *God: His Existence and His Nature*. 2 vols. St. Louis: B. Herder Book Co., 1936.

Gilson, Etienne. *The Philosophy of St. Thomas Aquinas*. Cambridge: W. Heffer and Sons, Ltd., 1929.

Hawkins, D. J. B. *Causality and Implication*. New York: Sheed and Ward, Inc., 1937.

Hick, John. *The Existence of God*. New York: The Macmillan Company, 1964.

———. *Philosophy of Religion*. Englewood Cliffs, N.J.: Prentice-Hall, Inc., 1962. Chapter 2.

Hicks, G. Dawes. *The Philosophical Basis of Theism*. New York: The Macmillan Company, 1937. Lectures 5 and 6.

Joyce, G. H. *The Principles of Natural Theology*. London: Longmans, Green and Co., 1924. Chap. 3.

Laird, John. *Theism and Cosmology*. New York: Philosophical Library and Alliance Book Corporation, 1942. Lectures 3 and 8.

Leibniz, G. W. *Theodicy*. Translated by E. M. Huggard. London: Routledge & Kegan Paul, 1952.

Maritain, Jacques. *Approaches to God*. Translated by Peter O'Reilly. New York: Harper and Brothers, 1954.

Mascall, E. L. *Existence and Analogy*. London: Longmans, Green and Co., 1949.

———. *He Who Is*. London: Longmans, Green and Co., 1943.

Matson, Wallace I. *The Existence of God*. Ithaca, N.Y.: Cornell University Press, 1965.

McTaggart, J. M. E. *Some Dogmas of Religion*. London: Arnold, 1906.

Pap, Arthur. *Elements of Analytic Philosophy*. New York: The Macmillan Company, 1949. Chapter 9.

Patterson, R. Leet. *The Conception of God in the Philosophy of Aquinas*. London: G. Allen & Unwin, Ltd., 1933.

Phillips, R. P. *Modern Thomistic Philosophy*. 2 vols. London: Burns, Oates & Washbourne, Ltd., 1935.

Russell, Bertrand. *Why I Am Not a Christian*. New York: Simon and Schuster, 1957.

Scriven, Michael. *Primary Philosophy*. New York: McGraw-Hill Book Company, 1966. Chapter 4.

Smith, Gerard. *Natural Theology*. New York: The Macmillan Company, 1951.

Smith, John E. *Philosophy of Religion*. New York: The Macmillan Company, 1965.

St. Augustine. *Confessions,* Book VII, Chapters 3–5, 12–16; *Enchiridion,* Chapters 3–5; *City of God,* Book XI, Chapters 1–9.

Tennant, F. R. *Philosophical Theology*. 2 vols. Cambridge: At The University Press, 1935.

Thompson, Samuel M. *A Modern Philosophy of Religion*. Chicago: Henry Regnery Co., 1955.

Whiteley, C. H. *An Introduction to Metaphysics*. London: Methuen & Co., Ltd., 1950.

ANCHOR BOOKS

Philosophy (continued)

ANCHOR BOOKS

Religion (continued)

ANCHOR BOOKS